SMALL THINGS,
BIG
THINGS

SMALL THINGS,
BIG
THINGS

INSPIRING STORIES OF EVERYDAY GRACE

MICHAEL A. MILTON

P U B L I S H I N G
P.O. BOX 817 • PHILLIPSBURG • NEW JERSEY 08865-0817

Typesetting and page design by Lakeside Design Plus

Printed in the United States of America

Library of Congress Cataloging-in-Publication Data

Milton, Michael A. (Michael Anthony), 1958–
    Small things, big things : inspiring stories of everyday grace / Michael A. Milton.
        p. cm.
    Includes bibliographical references.
    ISBN 978-1-59638-145-2 (pbk.)
    1. Grace (Theology)—Meditations. 2. Grace (Theology)—Anecdotes. 3. Christian life—Meditations. 4. Christian life—Anecdotes. I. Title.
BT761.3.M55 2009
234—dc22

                                                                2009038356

To the congregations I have served in Overland Park,
Savannah, and Chattanooga:
those sheep of the Good Shepherd,
who have sought his presence along craggy cliffs
and in pleasant pastures,
through all the seasons of our lives together.

To my little congregation at home,
Mae and John Michael,
gathered for our "Cotter's Saturday" nights,
where mother and father and son sought the Light
in the darkness,
not only for ourselves
but for the ones we felt called to serve.

To my Aunt Eva who worships Christ face to face.

And always, to my wife Mae.

"In your light do we see light."
—Psalm 36:9

"They said to each other, 'Did not our hearts burn within us while he talked to us on the road, while he opened to us the Scriptures?'"
—Luke 24:32

A prayer for this book and for those who read it:

> "May I always see Thy beauty with the clear eye of faith,
> and feel the power of Thy Spirit in my heart,
> for unless he move mightily in me
> no inward fire will be kindled."
> —A Puritan Prayer
> (*The Valley of Vision*, p. 187)

Contents

Contents

Contents

ACKNOWLEDGMENTS

I would like to thank Mr. Marvin Padgett with P&R Publishing, who first encouraged me in this project. He has been a great source of encouragement.

I am grateful to the saints at First Presbyterian Church of Chattanooga, Tennessee. I wrote most of these chapters for them, not for an audience somewhere "out there." I wrote for the faces of that congregation that came before me, in my mind's eye. I wrote for Wilma and Bill as they prayed for their son, John, in Iraq. I wrote for Scott and Carla as they cared for their aging parents. I wrote for Steve and Debbie, our colleagues in ministry. I wrote for Bill, who lost his precious wife way too soon. I wrote for Will, who was growing from a boy into an adolescent young man. I wrote for children like Sarah and young men like Seth. I wrote and thought of Bill, who led a major university. I wrote for Betty, who was a widow. I wrote for Cynthia, whose children were not walking with the Lord. I wrote for the mother of the child with Down Syndrome. I wrote for that child. I wrote for real people in a real place in a real time. I will never get you out of my mind or out of my heart. I thank you for allowing me to be your pastor. There is no higher honor than this.

I am grateful for Miss Helen Holbrook, who edited many of these little "messages" while she was the children's director at the church where I was pastor. When I accepted the call to become president of Reformed Theological Seminary in Charlotte, she came too. This work represents many hours of her time. Her own unfailingly helpful insights are embedded throughout. Thank you, Helen.

At First Presbyterian Church in Chattanooga I was blessed, during my time there, with two wonderful assistants. Mrs. Martha Miller had the gift of "helps" and combined that gift with a soft, Southern way of doing things that lifted my load and encouraged my soul. Mrs. April Gordon brought an extraordinary gift for efficiency to my office, as well as expert protection of my time. She also did all of these things with a graciousness and contagious humor that helped me in difficult times to laugh at myself and at the world. Thank you, April.

For the Reverend Steve Wallace and his wife, Debbie, I thank you for your friendship and counsel. Steve, you often reminded me, "Mike, you must focus on communicating the gospel." That gave me the freedom to write without guilt. Thank you, Steve.

Why do such acknowledgments invariably end with formal thanks to a spouse (for those of us who are married)? Is that just the proper form for such pages as this? It can be, I guess. But I think that beyond the technical and vocational gifts that create ministry and multiplication of ministry, all of which are vital and genuinely help form the writer and the writing, there is a person who shares in the deepest parts of life. That person is my wife, Mae. God's grace becomes clear to me by just being around her. Her spirituality is deeper than my own. Her gifts are not the gifts of teaching or administration or writing. Her gift is love. She has made our home a place of familial warmth and safe retreat. She is the consummate shepherd's wife. She welcomes me in from the rain and the snow as well as the blistering sun. She soothes my head, wipes my feet, and gives me food and drink. She nourishes my soul with words of encouragement and sometimes with the silent, comforting presence that speaks louder than words. She knows when to inquire about the state of the flock and when to say, "Why don't we just watch Andy Griffith and eat a piece of cake, honey." She brings joy and peace. She is God's gift to me. I thank her in a way that I thank no other person and in a way that would redefine, lengthen, and deepen the word *gratitude*.

INTRODUCTION

*T*he book you hold in your hands is a collection of little epistles written by a pastor to his people, but they are not sermons. They are musings, reflections, and sometimes critiques, but I wouldn't call them essays. They are each connected with spiritual things, most often scriptural subjects, but they are not devotionals. They are, I think, something else.

Once upon a time there was a wise mother who asked her two children as she tucked them into bed at night, "Where did you find God today?" The children, after a while of this, understood what their mother meant by these words that others, even adults, might find cryptic. One night her six-year-old boy said, "Momma, I found God when I fell down in the backyard and looked up and saw a cloud that looked like Uncle Purvis's nose." The mother smiled, nodded gently and approvingly, and said, "Very good." To her nine-year-old girl she asked, "And how about you?" And the daughter, wiser and more comfortable with her mother's game, said, "Momma, I saw God just now when you smiled out of the corner of your mouth, the way you do when you are satisfied with us." "Good," the mother replied. "Then you know he is with us." She would read a scripture, pray, tuck the children into bed, and turn out the light.

In a real way that is what these little pieces are. They are attempts by a father, a pastor, to help his congregation (often much wiser and more spiritually intuitive than their pastor, but maybe not with the time to sit and write about these things) to discover God's presence in the midst of their everyday lives. These theological reflections are my questions, embedded in stories and reflections and devotional thoughts, that are merely seeking to inquire, "Children, where did you find God today?" Then before they could answer, and in order that I might stir them to answer in their own way, I would seek to say, like that excited child, "I found him here! Let me tell you about it!"

I did this so that they would know that God is with us. I want them to know this in their minds and in their hearts, because as we travel through life together (and that is what pastor and people really do), we travel Wizard-of-Oz-like through the place of lions and tigers and bears. Or to use a more faithfully biblical metaphor, we travel like sheep down steep, narrow passageways that creep, dangerously high, alongside mountain ridges. When we are not high, we are low, traversing wilderness valleys where bitter waters flow and sinister wolves perch above us in the cliffs waiting for one of us, a pathetic weak one or a foolish strong one, to make a mistake and leave the flock.

The shepherd is there to calm the flock as well as to feed and protect them as they go along these pathways. Indeed, often they will not eat until they are calmed.

I have sought to do what the wise mother did with her questions. I really wanted my flock—Jesus' flock entrusted to me—to know that God is with us. Then we could move on and read his Word and pray and find our protection and our best nourishment as we looked up to see the true Shepherd in our midst.

I hope, in these pages, you too will begin to appreciate the goodness and grace of the God who comes to us in clouds that look like Uncle Purvis's nose, or in mincemeat pie that smells like home. Maybe you will say, "I am ready to find him too." If you do that, you will want to go further and say, "If I have found his glory in clouds and in aromas, what if I were to actually look into the clear Word he has left us? What if I were to sit at the feet of Jesus on a pleasant hillside in the gospel of John, or gather next to others in a crowded living room in Rome in the first century to hear an account of his life from St. Mark? What if I were to find him on a Roman cross being crucified by those whom he created, or teaching those who did not recognize him on the road to Emmaus?"

We are assured in the Bible that if we seek him, we will find him. These little chapters from a pastor's heart are here to nudge you to do just that. They are here to lead you to ask your own questions, make your own discoveries (which you will), and travel from discovering his grace in your own everyday life to discovering his grace in the unique life of Jesus of Nazareth. Then when you say "Aha! I saw him!" he will say to you, "My child, you discovered me because I led you there myself. You have seen because I have revealed myself to you." And that, my dear reader, is the greatest discovery of all.

_1_

WILL SNOOPER
BE IN HEAVEN?

_St. Francis, Eschatology,
and a Theology of Creation_

_The wolf shall dwell with the lamb, and the
leopard shall lie down with the young goat,
and the calf and the lion and the fattened calf
together; and a little child shall lead them._
—Isaiah 11:6

As you read through the newspaper in the spring
or the fall, you might come upon photographs
of the blessing of pets. If you are not familiar
with it, this is a service usually performed in Anglican
and Roman Catholic parishes. The service comes either

in the spring during Rogation days (the days following Easter and before Ascension Thursday) or in the fall (the Feast of St. Francis of Assisi). The members are encouraged to bring their kitties and puppies (in places like rural Wales they even bring their lambs) for a blessing by the priest or vicar. Some of us shun this for several reasons. One, is there really spiritual blessing or benefit conveyed by any act outside of faith? Two, do dogs and cats (and sheep and canaries) really need it?

The practice came about due to certain emphases in the church calendar and has developed over many years. It has roots in rural Britain where vicars made their way through lambing season or harvest time to ask God's blessing on animals and crops. In the Roman tradition, it is associated more with St. Francis, who is said to have spent much time in the woods "preaching" to the birds and, in general, giving thanks for creation.

The rite of the blessing of pets is growing in American Episcopal and Roman Catholic circles. However, most won't tell you, "I am bringing Rover to church because of Rogation Day" or "Because I, too, want to be associated with St. Francis's emphasis on thanking God for all of his creation, I bring my Tweety Bird." I suspect that most bring their pets to be blessed for other more sentimental reasons. I not only understand those reasons, I admit to the same sentiment.

Where am I going with this? The photos in the paper of the blessing of the pets coincided with a lengthy conversation I had in the car with my son while my wife was shopping (great theological discussions often happen while my wife is shopping). This conversation had to do with Snooper, and with Shadow, and with Tabby, and with eschatology, and with the hope in the heart of a little boy.

My son asked me a question that I bet most of you either asked as a child or have been asked by a child: will there be animals in heaven? My son wanted to know whether Shadow and Tabby would be in heaven. I think the conversation started because we talked about how our Welsh Corgi was getting older. This triggered not only a sadness in our midst at the thought of losing the little creature that had brought so much joy, but an opportunity to teach the Bible to my son.

"Well," I replied, looking for the words that would blend the truth of Scripture with the pastoral need in my son's life, "let me tell you about Snooper." Then I told the following story.

"Snooper was my childhood dog. A mongrel that looked like his ancestry could have included Welsh Corgis, Border Collies, German Shepherds, and Blue Tick hounds, Snooper was given to me on a cold winter morning when I was five years old. He came in a little cardboard box. Aunt Eva had told Osborn Turner, the famed school bus driver and hog farmer of Watson, Louisiana, that I sure could use a dog. I was an only child and coming out of some tough times as a little fellow, so Aunt Eva figured a puppy would help. This was long before psychology studies showed that pets help hurting kids and old folks. And Osborn found this pup.

"Aunt Eva would never allow a dog or cat or any other animal in the house, but she relented on this occasion because of the severe winter that year and the helplessness of that pup—or maybe because he was just downright cute! That little black and white pup began to grow, and he got into everything in sight. He spent most of his time snooping in the lower kitchen cabinets, and that was the reason Aunt Eva named him Snooper.

"Snooper and I grew up together. We ran through fields, chased lambs, got chased by bulls, got lost in cypress swamps, and he even went to school with me a few times. But eventually that little pup, who came to be my best friend, became very, very sick. I will never forget Dr. Smith, our veterinarian, coming out and pronouncing words that shook my world: "Son, Snooper is about to go to dog heaven." That last night of Snooper's life I slept with the old dog out in a shed in the back of the yard. I was about fifteen. When it was all over, I cried like anyone would. Like you probably will, son, when old Shadow finally goes. But I have a hope."

"You will see Snooper again?" my son asked.

"Well, I don't know how it all works, son, but God's Word says that creation—and that includes Snooper and Shadow and Tabby and all of the animals everywhere—is waiting for Jesus to come again. All of creation is waiting for a new heaven and a new earth."

I began to quote from Romans.

The created world itself can hardly wait for what's coming next. Everything in creation is being more or less held back. God reins it in until both creation and all the creatures are ready and can be released at the same moment into the glorious times ahead. Meanwhile, the joyful anticipation deepens. (Romans 8:19–21, MSG)

"So this is not all there is, for us or for creation," I told him. "And I know that the Bible tells us what that new day will be like for the world of animals.

> The wolf shall dwell with the lamb,
>> and the leopard shall lie down with the young goat,
> and the calf and the lion and the fattened calf together;
>> and a little child shall lead them. (Isaiah 11:6)

"God is on the move. Eden was lost through sin. But Jesus has redeemed us, and what he has done in our lives is now spreading through all the universe. One day everything will be brought fully under the lordship of Jesus, including creation. There is going to be a new heaven and a new earth, and it seems quite clear that since God originally made animals to provide companionship, even amusement, then they too will be redeemed."

"So I will see Shadow again?" he asked, wanting my Bible lesson to answer his deepest longing.

"Son, I know how you feel. I want to see Snooper again. All I know is that God made the animals, our pets, and God is going to renew all things. This is not the end. There is mystery, but there is great hope in the mystery of God's goodness."

About that time my wife came back to the car, and we drove home and talked some more. As we walked through the door, grocery bags in arm, we were greeted by wagging tails and contented purrs.

We are not planning to have any blessing of the pets per se, but we will stand with St. Francis of Assisi to say, "Thank you, Lord, for your gift of creation. It is wonderful. It is so like you to create a Welsh Corgi." We will, in a sense, go with the English vicars to the fields and say, "Lord, unless you bring the rain and the sun, there will be no crops. Unless you, O Lord, give protection to this ewe, there will be no lambs." We will acknowledge God's sovereign goodness in creation and our dependence upon him.

Little girls and boys and parents struggling for answers, come to the Lord and leave your hopes with him who made puppies and kittens and lambs and lions.

Yes, I sure would like to see old Snooper again. Who knows?

You know who.

2

GETTING THE CHICKENS
OUT OF THE RAIN

Take heart; it is I. Do not be afraid. — Mark 6:50

Y ou have all heard the expression, "Even a chicken has enough sense to come in out of the rain." That saying has been applied to me more than once. And when I consider Mark 6, about Jesus walking on the water and then coming into the disciples' boat to calm both the sea and their hearts, I am reminded of chickens coming in out of the rain— real chickens in real rain. In fact, I am thinking of biddies in the rain. Yes, biddies, as in chicks.

I was reared on a little chicken farm in South Louisiana. I began each day feeding chickens before school, and I ended each day gathering eggs. Believe it or not, I knew every one of those chickens by name. Every Buff Orpington, Golden Laced Wyandotte, Plymouth Barred

Rock (Aunt Eva's favorite: "good layers and they dress out real good too"), Rhode Island Red, and White Leghorn had a name. We didn't have as many as some of the great production farms, but we had a hundred or so.

One year—I was about ten years old—a spring flood came. The Amite River overflowed and all of the little tributaries were swollen beyond their banks. Beaver Creek, which ran through our property, flooded. The rising water began to creep into our yard and threaten our chickens, especially the spring biddies that were newly hatched and kept in a separate cage. I remember as if it were yesterday: Aunt Eva and I wading through the dirty water to get those chickens. It's a wonder a water moccasin didn't get us, because we were out there for a long time, scooping up chicks and, against the tide, hauling that biddie cage back to the house. We were blessed to save every one of them. We brought the biddies into the house and put them in my room. The chickens were herded (have you ever tried to herd chickens?), sacked up in burlap feed sacks, and left on the back porch. It was a mess, but that day a bunch of chickens experienced salvation.

As I was reading about how Jesus saved the disciples in the storm, I thought about how much like the biddies and chickens they were. I doubt if my biddies understood the figure of the old woman and the little boy wading through the water to get them. Maybe their cackling was like the screaming of the disciples when they saw the figure of the Master walking on the water. I know those biddies never thought about why we cared for them, but we did care. They were valuable to us. I couldn't explain it, but my concern went beyond dollar signs. I just loved those little biddies.

Jesus loved his disciples. He was like a parent, and he loved them. Mark tells us that they didn't "get it" when Jesus multiplied the loaves and fishes and fed the five thousand. They missed the deeper spiritual truth. And now they were alone and facing another crisis—still with little to no understanding about Jesus. He was the living bread they needed in their own lives. He was life to them and had everything they needed for every crisis they would ever face. But in the storm, in the rising water, as they were rowing against the wind, they didn't understand. In the end, it didn't matter that they had missed the deeper spiritual truth; Jesus' love for them went beyond their understanding. He saved them. They would figure it out later and then tell us about it.

Scholars tell us that early in the church's history, in the bloody killing fields of the persecutions and tribulations that Christians went through in Rome, pastors interpreted this passage in Mark to mean that Christ was with the martyrs. I think they interpreted it and applied it correctly. But will we? The point is this: even when you don't understand the person of Jesus, he is there walking on the water, passing by your little boat, coming to bring peace and salvation. Salvation does not depend upon you comprehending it all. Jesus will take care of that. We didn't ask the biddies to understand it all when we saved them from the flood, and Jesus won't require that of you. But in time, like the disciples and the early church, some of us will remember his figure in the storms we have faced and give thanks.

His salvation goes beyond understanding. All we recall is that when he came, we were saved. More insight will come. More faith will grow. But for now it is enough that the chickens are in out of the rain.

3

FROM LIVE OAK HARDWARE TO HEAVEN

We Are Going Somewhere

Then comes the end, when he delivers the kingdom to God the Father after destroying every rule and every authority and power. For he must reign until he has put all his enemies under his feet. . . . When all things are subjected to him . . . who put all things in subjection under him, that God may be all in all. —1 Corinthians 15:24–25, 28

We didn't have a car when I was growing up. We were stuck. That little hardscrabble farm was small and distant from the world I read about in books. Our only hope to "escape" (though there are times now when I would pay a great sum to escape back to that distant little place) was when someone would pick us up and take us to the big town of Watson (population about 500, counting cows). So when Aunt Eva would call out that we were going somewhere, I would get all excited. There was hope. Life wasn't just about the drudgery of feeding chickens and cows, gathering eggs, pulling turnips, or weeding fields. "We're going somewhere!" was a call to leap forward onto the broad sunlit uplands of a new world! It was about the excitement of the Live Oak Hardware and Feed Store—a new world for me every time I went there.

The Live Oak Hardware was, to me, like the British Museum holding rare and valuable treasures: shiny metallic plumbing fixtures, magnificent displays of seeds, and factory-fresh tools. If it was a really good day, I would see a new shipment of chicks packed tightly in their cardboard crates, or maybe the occasional new tractor parked out front (candy apple red Massey-Fergusons, crab apple green John Deeres, and sky blue Fords). I can still smell the feed in the feed sacks out back. When no one was looking, I would hop from one sack to another, not caring if I fell, for to fall on those sacks was to fall onto the soft but slightly scratchy burlap and smell the corn and oats all mixed together.

The Red and White Grocery, right across the road from Live Oak Hardware, offered its seemingly endless aisles of brightly colored canned goods. (Now that I think about it, there were only about four aisles.) Every now and then the meat section would offer fish, and when the meat cutter wasn't looking, I would reach out and experience what a red snapper felt like. I loved it when there were samples of the latest cereal or ice cream flavor. I loved to read the backs of the cans or the packages to see where the produce came from. Somehow, by holding a package of food from Florida or by cradling cans from Kansas City, I was in touch with the big wide world out there. With my imagination, a global vision could be cultivated from the Red and White Grocery. I still love going to grocery stores. Just ask my wife. I am like a wide-eyed child from the backwoods who doesn't often get to see such sights.

When I was a boy, going somewhere also meant seeing and interacting with people. I loved Aunt Eva, but it was nice when we got to see more people than just the two of us. So when I heard her calling out, "Son, we are going somewhere today!" I would drop that feed bucket, leave that rake in the turnip field, and put those dirty bare feet into high gear.

We are going somewhere. We are a people on our way. We are going to that fantastic moment when ultimate redemption through the defeat of death will open graves, dry tears, and bring reunion.

We are going to a date that is fixed in the mind and plan of Almighty God when paradise lost will become paradise restored and the longing of the ages will be wondrously satisfied.

We are going to a day when all other powers will be subdued under the cosmic grace of God in Christ, and every knee shall bow.

We are going to a most amazing event when our Savior, having completed his work from beginning to end and received all of the elect of God, will present these trophies of his grace to his Father.

We are going to a time when, after thousands of redemptive years to us but a few seconds to God, the new heaven and the new earth will begin.

Let the certainty of God's work give you courage. Let the revelation of God put a lilt in your step and a smile on your face. Let the glorious thought comfort you in your trials. Let the cosmic plan of God, now revealed to his people in his Word, lift your head out of your troubles. Let the promise encourage you in a vocation that may have become drudgery. Let the reality turn you to Jesus who invites you to come.

We are going somewhere, and the population is far greater than Watson, Louisiana. It will be far more spectacular than even the Live Oak Hardware or the Red and White Grocery. It will be out of this world, and it will never end. Never.

Yes, we are really going somewhere. And if you see it through the eyes of eternity, you just might say, "We are almost there."

4

INDEPENDENCE DAY
OF THE SOUL

S ir Edwin Arnold (1832–1904) wrote, "Within yourself deliverance must be searched for, because
each man makes his own prison."[1]
That is a lie.

Sir Edwin Arnold, a contemporary of the great Scottish medical missionary David Livingston (1813–1873),
dabbled in the teachings of Buddha, and this attractive
lie reflects his personal syncretism of Christ and Buddha. It is true that man without God is in a prison, but
it is a prison whose first cell is constructed by the corruption of original sin. We are born in this state. The
classical Augustinian understanding of human nature,
grounded in God's Word, is a help to us at this point.

1. http://www.answers.com/topic/edwin-arnold

Pre-Fallen Man: It is possible for man to sin and possible for him not to sin (*posse peccare et posse non peccare*).

Adam chose sin and fell, and in his falling, mankind, like it or not, was associated with him and born into sin. That leads to the second condition of man, and this is the real prison.

Fallen Man: Man is not able not to sin (*non posse non peccare*).

Humanism, which can be described as claiming that the freedom of the soul may be found within the human soul itself, was championed by Desiderius Erasmus of Rotterdam (1466–1536). Erasmus's theology of man was that man is free to choose his own way out of the mess he is in—a philosophy championed in his popular humanist manifesto *The Freedom of the Will* (1524). Martin Luther, who understood both what God revealed in the Bible and what experience itself teaches, countered Erasmus's book with his own.

Luther's book was sarcastically but accurately called *The Bondage of the Will* (1525). Man without regeneration, man left to himself, is incarcerated in a humanly impenetrable prison. He is born into that prison, for his mother and father were also inmates (Psalm 51:5). Luther might have agreed with Sir Edwin when he said that each man makes his own prison, but Luther said that is not the whole story. Man makes his prison because his will is in prison. The heart of man without God fosters sin, and even when he does good, his motives are sinful. "The heart is deceitful above all things and beyond cure. Who can understand it?" (Jeremiah 17:9, NIV)

Even when man's motives are pure in his own eyes, they are sin in the eyes of his Creator because he does not acknowledge God (Jeremiah 9:3). Man is sinful through and through. This is what Luther meant. It is what the Bible means when it says that a man's righteousness is like filthy rags. It is what Jesus meant when he told the Pharisees that though they could claim lineage to Abraham and though they could make a show of outwardly good works, they were truly of their father, the devil. It is what Paul meant when he said that all have sinned and fallen short of the glory of God. Man without God is incarcerated by his own sin. That is the state of people without God today. It will take what Luther called "an alien righteousness" to transform this condition.

Once long ago, I sat alone in a military barracks in San Angelo, Texas, with a bottle and a glass. I hated the taste of whiskey, could never drink more than a few sips of it, but it seemed to be the thing to do for a young man who felt so alone, so isolated, so enchained. Drunkenness would have provided some escape, but I could never get past the burning and choking. So I sat in stone cold sobriety staring into the bottle. I am not sure which would have been worse: drunken disillusionment or sober sadness. Why was I in this position? I wanted freedom . . . freedom from myself. I was nineteen years old and was in my own prison. Unhappy, unsure, dissatisfied, and discouraged. There may be someone reading this who feels just that way.

Knowing that I had to be free, I struggled to a new position; I became a very religious man. But by age twenty-three I found that I was still in prison. The darkened barracks and bottle had been replaced by a stained glass window and a lot of religious knowledge. But the inner feelings, the confusion, were still there. Maybe some of you reading this are looking into a mirror. A man is imprisoned unless and until that remarkable light from heaven transforms his soul. The bottle is slow suicide that kills you and hurts everyone around you. Religion is a pall draping the casket of a dying soul, a hypocritical sham that has no ability to breathe life into your own soul or to touch the soul of another. Freedom can only come from Luther's "alien righteousness"—a divine outside force. For a man cannot produce what he does not have to begin with. And so I was enchained. I was in the state of the Fallen Man: it was not possible for me not to sin.

Coming to know of God's wondrous grace in Jesus Christ transformed me. The alien righteousness of Jesus Christ was imputed to my sinful soul. His blood covered my original and actual sin. I was born again. I became:

Regenerated Man: It is possible for man to sin and possible for him not to sin (*posse peccare et posse non peccare*).

In other words, in Christ we are returned to the pre-fall condition of man. And here we are released from our prison. Through Jesus Christ alone we come to know true freedom. My fear was replaced with blessed assurance. My guilt was removed through his promise of forgiveness sealed with his death on the cross and his great cry, "It is finished!" My sadness was overwhelmed by a joy that I had never known and a joy that is now wonderfully familiar to me. It is a joy that has been implanted. It is not an emotion, but it produces an emotion. This joy, this reality, can only be the life of Jesus Christ now living in me.

We cannot find freedom within ourselves. It is not there. Freedom that liberates the human soul comes only from the one who created our souls. We search in all the wrong places if we search for freedom apart from the Light of the World, Jesus Christ.

Jesus said, "Then you will know the truth, and the truth will set you free. . . . So if the Son sets you free, you will be free indeed" (John 8:32, 36 NIV). I love the way Charles Haddon Spurgeon put it: "I do not come into this pulpit hoping that perhaps somebody will, of his own free will, return to Christ—that may be so or not—but my hope lies in another quarter. I hope that my Master will lay hold of some of them and say, 'You are mine and you shall be mine. I claim you for myself.' My hope arises from the freeness of grace—not from the freedom of the will!"[2] Our freedom in Christ is leading us to a more glorious freedom. It is our final state of being.

Glorified Man. Man is not able to sin (*non posse peccare*).

This is the state of our Lord Jesus. It is the state of our mothers and fathers in the faith who have gone before us. They are perfected, glorified, completed. What God has started, he has now, in their lives, completed. Death for the believer ushers us into the fullest expression of humanity and life: finally being free from even the temptation to sin.

2. C.H. Spurgeon, "Other Sheep and One Flock," sermon number 1713, delivered at the Metropolitan Tabernacle, Newington, March 25, 1883. Available online at http://www.spurgeongems.org/vols28-30/chs1713.pdf.

Perhaps the saddest condition is frolicking in the cell of sin and thinking that it is freedom. That condition is like an inmate dancing in the cell and calling himself free before being led to the electric chair, or perhaps worse, an eternity of solitary confinement.

My independence day was many years ago when God, by his mere grace, walked into the dark corner of my cell and freed me. Charles Wesley's independence day was in another era. In 1738 he wrote his first hymn, and these words shall always stir me to praise.

> Long my imprisoned spirit lay,
> Fast bound in sin and nature's night;
> Thine eye diffused the quickening ray—
> I woke, the dungeon flamed with light;
> My chains fell off, my heart was free,
> I rose, went forth, and followed Thee.[3]

And there is the glorious paradox. Paul described well what I have become when he wrote, "You have been set free from sin and have become slaves to righteousness" (Romans 6:18, NIV). My Master is my friend, and in his velvet chains I have truly found my freedom.

May all who read these words truly know the freedom, the ultimate freedom that comes from the life of Jesus Christ living in you. May none of you go away without claiming your independence from sin. And you can't find it by looking within, Sir Arnold. You are "fast bound in sin." The only way to claim freedom is to lay hold of the free grace of God offered by faith in Jesus Christ.

---

3. Charles Wesley, "And Can It Be," available online at http://www.cyberhymnal.org/htm/a/c/acanitbe.htm.

5

GRACE IN WINTER

*I*n my yard, the passing of autumn not only deposits piles of leaves, it also reveals points of neglect. When there is no foliage on my trees and plants, I begin to see areas that I missed with the lawnmower. I notice beds that need mulching, hedges that need fertilizing, perennials that need tending, and new plants that need watering. Once, under barren twigs, I even found some old gloves I had left behind on a long-forgotten workday. Or did they belong to the homeowner before me, the other bird who has flown and in whose nest I now make my home? I don't know. But, with each passing autumn and approaching winter, because of the barrenness of the trees and plants, I discover problems in my yard.

The winter seasons of life also remove the foliage of happier, more carefree days. The winter of our lives reveals areas of neglect in our souls: days when we forgot to hide God's Word in our hearts, when we spent more time with the television than with God in prayer, when we rushed through the day without investing time in our families or thoughtful reflection.

The coming of Thanksgiving every year is for me a time to re-center my life on gratitude to God and his Son Jesus Christ. It is a time to fertilize my heart with remembrances of his grace, reflect on his goodness and mercy, and slow down again and remember that my days are numbered. For this I am thankful. I am thankful for Thanksgiving itself. Above and beyond the warmth and beauty of family and friends gathered, there is the event of giving thanks to God, remembering him, and cleaning up the missed spots of life by taking all things to him in prayer.

Winter will come this year as it always does, but my beds will be mulched. My plants will be fertilized. My old stuff will be picked up and put away. I will get ready for winter. I will prepare for spring. I will enter the season with Thanksgiving.

6

It Takes a Church

*Our Commitment to a
Christian Worldview for our Children*

*You shall love the L*ORD *your God with
all your heart and with all your soul and
with all your might. And these words that
I command you today shall be on your
heart. You shall teach them diligently to
your children, and shall talk of them when
you sit in your house, and when you walk
by the way, and when you lie down, and
when you rise. You shall bind them as
a sign on your hand, and they shall be
as frontlets between your eyes. You shall
write them on the doorposts of your house
and on your gates. —Deuteronomy 6:5–9*

*Like arrows in the hand of a warrior are the
children of one's youth. —Psalm 127:4*

*And all who believed were together and had
all things in common. —Acts 2:44*

J ohn Knox knew how to reform the church.
When he wanted to bring the gospel of grace
to every inch of Scotland and desired that
the church be conformed in doctrine, government,
and worship to the Word of God, he wrote this basic
philosophy of ministry: "Seeing that God hath determined that his Church here on earth shall be taught
not by angels but by men; . . . it is necessary . . . [to]
be most careful for the virtuous education and godly
upbringing of the youth of this realm."[1] The secret to
long-term reformation is the rearing of a godly line.
And Knox's influence succeeded! Indeed, many of us
trace our ancestry to Scots who were influenced by
the credo, "Rear up a godly line and you will secure
the future you desire."

Some time ago, Hillary Clinton wrote a book entitled *It Takes a Village*. The book reflected her views
that community is needed in the rearing of children. I
take many and great exceptions with her view of "community," but I cannot disagree with the premise that
bringing up children, while it is first and foremost the
work of the family, must be supported by the larger

1. John Knox, The History of the Reformation of the Religion of Scotland
(included in *Knox's Confession* and *Book of Discipline*), p. 382. Available
online at http://www.holybible.com/resources/living_learning/fall_1999/
knox_and_calvin.htm.

community. When I look at Deuteronomy 6, I see this truth taught, but I would not say that it takes a village. I would say that it takes a church—a local, covenanted assembly of Bible-saturated, Christ-centered, gospel-and-grace-gripped people who look into the eyes of children and see God's potential for the future they envision for his glory. As they look into those eyes, they feel the burden of God's Word and the presence of history being written.

I thought about this as my wife and I received a video from Westminster Academy, a school I founded in Overland Park, Kansas. The school is flourishing, and the testimonies on camera—the faces and the voices of little children—moved us to tears. It seems like yesterday (it was only 1993) that I left Ft. Lauderdale to return to the Kansas City area. I rented a room at the Marriott Hotel and told a gathering that if we hoped to see emerge the kind of leaders who founded this nation, and if we dreamed of a time when young men and women would possess a worldview that would bring Christ's truth to bear in every endeavor of life, then we would have to be intentional about rearing up such a generation. We needed to do this not only as individual Christians, but also collectively, as a new community. One way, I proposed, was through the establishment of a church and a school. It still seems like a bad joke when I think of the man whom God was using to speak those things, but that dream, that idea—even coming from the life of a broken man like me—flowered in remarkable ways. Though God led me, after five years of ministry there, to leave and teach seminary students and then to plant another church before finding my place of service at First

Presbyterian Church in Chattanooga, you can understand how my heart is moved to see the success of that ministry back in Kansas. For behind the expanded numbers and twenty-acre campus and new buildings, there are the lives of those precious faces. I see young leaders—homemakers, teachers, tradesmen, writers, statesmen, business people, ministers, and moms and dads—standing up with a radically biblical worldview to take on the giants of the future with faith in the ruling and reigning Christ.

I write to emphasize this point: we must do all, give all, and focus all on rearing up, in the church, a group of children who will have a distinctive world and life view, a view that Christ is Lord of the arts as well as the sciences. We must raise children with a worldview that Jesus Christ is Lord of the home and Lord of the marketplace, and with a worldview that values homemakers as well as presidents and honest laborers as well as physicians. All of that must begin with a high view of God's Word, a strong grounding in the doctrines of the Word of God, and a compassionate, broken heart for the lost. The children and youth staff in our churches are vital to this. But we need more than staff. We must have committed families and concerned men and women of God who will stand in the gap for this generation. We pray not only for children to have biblical and theological knowledge, but first and foremost that they will have a love of Jesus and a heart for Jesus' rule and reign in our society. I pray that we may shoot arrows out into the future that will be change agents in this world.

One Sunday morning during the greeting time at our church, a little child personally handed me his pledge card. It was for $50. It moved me deeply. That child had heard the testimony of one of our members from the pulpit, and the Spirit had moved him to give of what he didn't even have yet. But he trusted God for the future.

Let's trust God for the future. Let's pledge our little ones in the church to the Lord. You may be married with no children. You may be single. But we are the covenanted community of Jesus Christ in this place. These children are your children, in some sense. They are your future, in some way. Together we are his people praying for revival and reformation in our nation. May God raise up a godly line out of our generation. What we need are men and women who dream of tomorrow and whose dreams of renewal cause them to pray, teach, and give time, talents, and tithes while they model a Christian worldview for our children to see. What we must have are congregations that see their children as a heritage from the Lord and view the work of the church as preparing these little ones to be shot out like sacred arrows into the future to change the world for Jesus Christ.

What are you doing to encourage families? What are you doing to encourage a little child you see on Sunday mornings? How are you supporting the work of your church to uphold its mission to assist parents in the Christian nurturing of their children? It really does "take a church."

7

LASER SURGERY FOR MY DIM VISION

That the God of our Lord Jesus Christ, the
Father of glory, may give you a spirit of
wisdom and of revelation in the knowledge
of him. —Ephesians 1:17

Not long ago, I was having a conversation about laser surgery and how it has transformed our lives. In particular, I was discussing cataract surgery, which used to be such an ordeal, but now has become a relatively routine procedure. I know there are many people who thank God for laser surgery.

Shortly thereafter, at the National Conference on Preaching, I was reminded that preachers can get cataracts of the soul and forget that our main work, according to God's Word, is the work of preaching. Preaching the Word of God is the divinely ordained surgical procedure that removes the cataracts from our souls. To be precise and effective, like laser surgery, preaching must be radically biblical, conveying the mind of God to every generation. To direct that laser, there must be consecrated time of study and meditation on the Word, as well as personal conviction of that Word in the preacher's own soul.

John Calvin wrote, on the book of Ephesians,

> But what does Paul wish for the Ephesians? *The spirit of wisdom, and the eyes of their understanding being enlightened.* And did they not possess these? Yes; but at the same time they needed increase, that, being endowed with a larger measure of the Spirit, and being more and more enlightened, they might more clearly and fully hold their present views. The knowledge of the godly is never so pure, but that some dimness or obscurity hangs over their spiritual vision. (emphasis in original)[1]

"Dimness" and "obscurity" are the spiritual cataracts that must be removed for the Spirit to flow in my life and in yours.

I went to this conference to teach others about the surgical procedure known as expository preaching. In the midst of it the Lord showed me that I had a cataract or two that needed to go. As I sat under the preaching of expositors such as Dr. Bryan Chapell and Dr. Al Mohler, I experienced much-needed repairs.

Mohler reminded us (according to my notes and recollection) that preaching is irrelevant and out of date in the minds of postmodern man. In our country

1. John Calvin, *Commentary on Galatians and Ephesians*, available online at http://www.ccel.org/ccel/calvin/calcom41.iv.ii.iv.html.

the preacher once held a standing with other professionals, but no more. We who believe in the power of the Word are odd in the context of modern life. Our message is not conditioned by what people want, but by what God demands. Postmodern people want to be told something interesting, not that there is truth in the propositional, inerrant, and infallible Word of God that demands a response. Postmodern man wants something he can think about at lunch and forget by dinner. But expository preaching goes out on a limb. It makes bold proclamations about man and God, and about how all Scripture beats a beeline to the cross. Yes, we are out of step and odd, and we are not tame anymore. That is good. Tamed Christianity got us to where we are today. Some think we are even dangerous in our culture. Good. Preaching needs to be dangerous, for God's Word is dangerous.

A whole sanctuary of preachers sat still while not a few cataracts rolled onto the floor. We who sat under the preaching that night realized again that handling the Word of God is a dangerous matter for the preacher as well as the listener. And that night we were hearing, growing, having the eyes of our hearts opened. I thank God for that.

I hurried back to my dorm room and called my family and told them that I had just heard heaven thunder through great preaching. I told them that I was glad I had heard the Word that night, and that I was humbled to be a preacher. I went to sleep praying that I may see afresh the calling of God in my life—to know the glory of Christ in Scripture so that I may better preach his majesty and rest assured in his Word.

Each week I pray that the message of God's Word will penetrate the hearts of my congregation as I preach. I trust that your pastor does the same. I ask that you pray that it will penetrate his in turn—that he will not only preach the message of the given text, but also deliver it according to the way the Spirit delivers it in the Bible. Pray that he will really get the message the Spirit is recording and then deliver that message faithfully. For there is no other way for people to be saved than through the Word of God, and there is no other way for Christians to grow than through the Word of God. All of us, especially preachers, need the laser surgery of the Word. We need to see clearly the glory of God in the Word of God.

8

A Theology
of Mincemeat Pie

I grew up eating mincemeat pies. Aunt Eva made them every Christmas, and as a child, I loved those pies. They were made of a finely chopped, cooked mixture that included raisins, currants, apples, suet, sugar, spice, candied peel, and often meat, brandy or cider, and other ingredients. Mincemeat pies were as much a part of my Christmas sensory experience as the scent of a Christmas tree freshly cut from our pasture and the sight of cheap, festive lights just purchased from Live Oak Hardware in Watson, Louisiana.

But later I grew tired of mincemeat. I am not sure if it was the spices that got to me or if it was the coating that clung to my palate several hours after having eaten one. Mae remembers my informing her soon after we were married, "Aunt Eva still thinks I like mincemeat pies for Christmas; the truth is, I do not like them at all. I am tired of them." In fact, until one night recently, just outside the village of Tobermory on the Isle of Mull in Scotland, I do not think I had tasted mincemeat pie since my grace awakening in Jesus Christ in 1985.

We had eaten our dinner that evening in the beautiful little fishing village with the strange name. The night was velvet black as we were winding our way back to our hotel. There was a trace of moonlight squeezing through the low-pitched Hebridean clouds. The seemingly ancient roads were narrowed to one lane. The endless flocks of sheep were grazing nonchalantly on roadside grass. Suddenly my wife yelled, "Stop!" I slammed on the brakes!

You probably think that I was about to hit a sheep, but that was not it at all. A craft store had suddenly appeared just to our right. My wife had a woman's intuition that this out-of-the-way little shop could be just the chosen spot where she would find a certain craft item she had been looking for. I threw the car into a slide across some gravel and turned in. No sooner had we parked our borrowed Volvo, its tires still smoking from the abrupt stop and the sheep unmoved but safe, than my wife found her prize.

As she and John Michael continued to look over the crafts, I noticed that the upstairs part of the shop had been turned into a little café. Wanting to satisfy my sweet tooth after dinner, I decided to climb the stairs and look around. It was there, as I gazed through the glass case of assorted pastries, that I spotted the little sign: "Mincemeat pies freshly prepared." I had not thought about mincemeat in a long time, but deep inside I knew that one was now going to be mine. I wanted to learn why I had loved mincemeat as a child and why I had turned against it as a young adult. The cost was only a pound, so even if I still hated it, it would have been worth it to say that I had eaten a piece of mincemeat pie.

I did eat the pie, and I loved it. Like a child who had found a long lost friend, I ran down and told Mae, "It's mincemeat." She glanced over and said, "But you don't like mincemeat." It was then that I announced, "But something has happened. I do like mincemeat pie. I love it. It is wonderful. Just look at those apples and raisins and orange peel and those chopped nuts and all of that other unidentifiable stuff in there!"

Then I said it—and as I said it, I knew something deeper than pie was happening inside me. "Honey, it reminds me of something . . . something good . . . something warm . . . let's see, how can I say it?" I paused, pondering the connection between my heart and my palate. "I know. Mincemeat pie reminds me of Christmas."

Since then I have thought more and more about mincemeat pie and the meaning of that moment. Perhaps my dislike of mincemeat pie was due to the ordinary shifts in tastes that happen to all of us as we move from one stage of life to another. Or perhaps my prodigal journey away from the things of God and away from the Christ of Christmas caused me to lose my taste for mincemeat. In the same way some people say that you cannot eat peanut butter and jelly sandwiches and be depressed or chew bubble gum and be serious, I could not eat mincemeat pie—so intertwined in my mind with Christmas and the wonder of faith—without the guilt associated with my distance from Jesus.

Sin sears the taste for beauty. What we once cherished when we walked with God, we casually chuck when we walk with the world. Gifts we once held as sacred under the umbrella of Christian influence, we throw away as worthless under the sinister power of sin's sway. What we once held close to our breast as treasure in innocent days, we uncaringly discard as rubbish in wicked times.

Sin had taken much from me on my wayfaring journey into the far country. Lives, relationships, years, potential, prospects, happiness, and so much more were left with the hogs and the pods in that faraway land of wasted living. By the grace of God, I came home, and God granted me a new life—a new taste for living. Jesus does that. The Lord told the sinning people of God, "So I will restore to you the years that the swarming locust has eaten" (Joel 2:25a, NKJV). God used that mincemeat pie as a small reminder of the warmth of home and the serenity of mind and spirit that had been given back to me by his grace.

I went back up the stairs to the little café and stood in line to get the last piece of mincemeat pie in the glass case! But others were ahead of me, and my family— the real testimony to his goodness in restoring what the locust had eaten—waited for me downstairs. I did not have to cling to the last piece of mincemeat pie after all. I could leave it. I had found something that had been lost. I had been reminded of the promises of God. It was enough now to remember the words of the psalmist and believe them and rejoice in them.

> The poor will eat and be satisfied;
>> they who seek the LORD will praise him—
>> may your hearts live forever! (Psalm 22:26, NIV)

> How sweet are your words to my taste,
>> sweeter than honey to my mouth!
>> (Psalm 119:103)

9

PRAYER FOR A
BROKEN HEART

For even his own brothers did not believe in
him. —John 7:5, NIV

"P reach to those with a broken heart and you will
never lack for a congregation," one older and wiser
pastor instructed me. I believe he is right.

Dear Brother and Sister:

Your family is divided by unbelief. Is it your husband?
Your wife? Or, like our Lord, your brothers? Or is it,
O broken mother, O grieving father, your baby boy?
He made you so proud when he memorized the Scriptures and got the award. Now you have watched him
go through a divorce, juggle weekend visits with his
children, and sink deeper into depression and unbelief.

Or is it your baby girl? Now she is twenty-one and struggling beneath a cunning professor's dissection of everything you taught her. She is falling, falling away. You know it and you feel that every time you bring up the matter, it only elicits pain—pain and distance. You want her closer now than ever, and you hurt for her. You are confused. You know how you reared her.

Now you come to me, your pastor, and what can I tell you? "Chin up, it will be all right?" I dare not trivialize deep waters with little droplets of axioms. The gospel is deep enough, Christ is Savior enough, and God's patience and love are long enough and wide enough to hold you while you pray and hope and wait. "Love believes all things," and I will stand with you in believing this. I will stand with you in prayer and believe that your son, in his heartache, will find healing. I will believe with you that your daughter will come to see the superiority of happy faith in a living Lord over grim skepticism in intriguing but lifeless ideas. I will stand with you to pray, "Lord, as your resurrection brought conversion to your family, will you so shine your life through your son, your daughter, so that their children may see you? Will you, Lord Jesus, give them hope to see through the fog of despair to trust you for their children's salvation?" I do pray that. And I want you to do something. I want you to recall that you and your unsaved loved one must pray the same prayer. For in coming so close to their unbelief, you have started to doubt yourself. So pause and pray the biblical prayer that admits the ambiguity you face: "Lord, I believe; help thou mine unbelief" (Mark 9:24, KJV).

This is your prayer. This is their prayer. This prayer admits that there are questions remaining, but it also surrenders the questions to the one who has the answers.

Live the gospel in your prayers. Don't flaunt your faith before your unsaved loved one, but love them through it. Let the grace that saved you live through you. In your weakness you are made strong. I have no other answers. Pray. Believe. Hope. Witness from your brokenness.

The one who writes this is one who has been prayed for and brought home to the joy of Christ Jesus by such prayers, such faith, such hope, and such simple witness. I pray with you. Much more importantly, Jesus is your mediator, and I have hope in him and his love for your loved ones. He loves them more than you do, and his love is unsearchable. He will reach them as he reached his own family. Please smile. And don't give up.

Your pastor and friend,
Mike

10

SMALL THINGS, BIG THINGS, APRONS, AND HEAVEN

*They were longing for a better country
—a heavenly one. Therefore God is not
ashamed to be called their God, for he has
prepared a city for them. —Hebrews 11:16,
NIV*

Peggy Noonan, Ronald Reagan's speechwriter, wrote about how the big things in life are best expressed through simple things. The small things get at the deeper things in powerful ways. To be sure, there are great and magnificent things, other stories, lurking beneath the smaller and more obvious stories of our lives. Common things, powerful things. Small words, big things.

Recently a small word helped me meditate on a big idea as it uncovered a deeper story. The small word is "apron." The big concept is "home." The deeper story is "heaven."

I had not thought about Aunt Eva's apron for a long time when I read an article about aprons.

The principal use of Grandma's apron was to protect the dress underneath, but along with that it served as a holder for removing hot pans from the oven. It was wonderful for drying children's tears, and on occasion was even used for cleaning out dirty ears.

From the chicken-coop the apron was used for carrying eggs, fussy chicks, and sometimes half-hatched eggs to be finished in the warming oven.

When company came, those aprons were ideal hiding places for shy kids, and when the weather was cold, grandma wrapped it around her arms.

Those big old aprons wiped many a perspiring brow bent over the hot wood stove. Chips and kindling wood were brought into the kitchen in that apron.

From the garden, it carried all sorts of vegetables. After the peas had been shelled, it carried out the hulls.

In the fall, the apron was used to bring in apples that had fallen from the trees. When unexpected company drove up the road, it was surprising how much furniture that old apron could dust in a matter of seconds.

When dinner was ready, Grandma walked out onto the porch, waved her apron, and the men knew it was time to come in from the fields to dinner.

It will be a long time before someone invents something that will replace that "old-time apron" that served so many purposes.[1]

This is the clearest picture of my Aunt Eva's apron I have ever read. I wiped my nose on that apron many times! She carried many a little chick in that apron, and I can still see her wiping off the kitchen counter with it (did I wipe my nose before or after the biddies and the countertop?).

As you read this, many of you thought of your mother, grandmother, or another of God's saints sent to love and care for you. Why do we respond so emotionally to things like aprons? The apron is a small thing, but there is a bigger thing behind it; there is another story. Just as a song from a long ago courtship can rekindle romance for a married couple, aprons and other small things can create a longing for that big thing called home.

Thomas Wolfe said, "You can never go home again." There is truth in Wolfe's famous line. The apron produces a longing, but it is almost cruel in its emotive power, for such nostalgic longings cannot lead us back home. The home we remember is not there. The apron is no more. In my case, the one who wore the apron is not there. Do such things just produce unrequited longings? Sadness? What are they worth if that is all they do? For those who have no hope of heaven, nostalgia is a bittersweet experience that leads to emptiness—like the four-year-old child who stood before the Christmas tree two days afterward and cried, "Is that all there is?"

1. http://ezinearticles.com/?Grandmas-Apron---Author-Unknown&id=63999.

But lo, I show you a mystery. There is another story. For the one who is journeying through this life to a place called home, the small things that warm our hearts, that rekindle good memories, and inevitably stir longings, are God-sent moments to make us long for the really big thing: our home with the Lord Jesus Christ. Every sunset we can never forget, every fond memory from childhood, every crumbling flower marking a special page in a childhood book, every puppy love—in short, every apron—is God beckoning, "You are not home, but home is where I am taking you. Let the apron string that is tugging at your heartstring remind you! I am your home. You are not there now, my child, but you are getting closer."

> You trust God, don't you? Trust me. There is plenty of room for you in my Father's home. If that weren't so, would I have told you that I'm on my way to get a room ready for you? And if I'm on my way to get your room ready, I'll come back and get you so you can live where I live. (John 14:1–3, MSG)

Small things. Big things. Another story. Aprons. Home. Heaven. It's all getting clearer.

11

THE BEAUTY OF THE RADIANT CITY OF GOD IN THE GRANITE GRAY CITIES OF MAN

*I*n Revelation 21, we read of the revelation of Jesus to his churches. We read earthly words about earthly images to describe a city that is literally out of this world. As you read, your mind conjures up the most amazingly brilliant and dazzling vista ever beheld. It is pure beauty!

> The wall was made of jasper, and the city of pure gold, as pure as glass. The foundations of the city walls were decorated with every kind of precious stone. The first foundation was jasper, the second sapphire, the third chalcedony, the fourth emerald, the fifth sardonyx, the sixth carnelian, the seventh chrysolite, the eighth beryl, the ninth topaz, the tenth

chrysoprase, the eleventh jacinth, and the twelfth amethyst. The twelve gates were twelve pearls, each gate made of a single pearl. The great street of the city was of pure gold, like transparent glass.

I did not see a temple in the city, because the Lord God Almighty and the Lamb are its temple. The city does not need the sun or the moon to shine on it, for the glory of God gives it light, and the Lamb is its lamp. The nations will walk by its light, and the kings of the earth will bring their splendor into it. On no day will its gates ever be shut, for there will be no night there. The glory and honor of the nations will be brought into it. Nothing impure will ever enter it, nor will anyone who does what is shameful or deceitful, but only those whose names are written in the Lamb's book of life. (Revelation 21:18–27, NIV)

I thought about these verses while I was in Aberdeen, Scotland. Aberdeen is called the Granite City of Scotland because it is nearly all granite! That means the entire city seems to be colored battleship granite gray. Add that gray to the many days of low-hanging gray cloud cover, a little drizzly rain which also seems to be a translucent ashen color, and the perennial blue-gray, hazy, thick sea mist coming in from the adjacent North Sea, and you've got a gray environment. Our little holiday flat was only a short walk from the sea, and the sea gulls seemed to mourn over this spectacle all night long. The whole of it could actually cause one to become quite depressed.

But there is something beautiful about Aberdeen. Can you believe that this city of granite gray is also called the City of Flowers? Yes, it is! Roses of every color and a spectacular array of wildflowers are like the multicolored stones of the walls of the New Jerusalem. The colors of the flowers are all the more brilliant against the granite gray backdrop of misty Aberdeen. And when the sun comes out, you have never seen such clear, undiluted color and beauty! It is this sight and this contrast that gripped my attention.

This world can be granite gray as we look at all of the sin, the shame, the guilt, and the tragic consequences of rebellion against God, all standing granite-like against the goodness of God. Overwhelmed by the disorienting sea mists of a vast depth of unrighteousness, we, like the sea birds in Aberdeen, sometimes mourn the sight. But the grace of God shown in Jesus Christ shines all the brighter when placed in front of such a sinful backdrop. Where sin abounds, grace abounds much more.[1] Thus the city of man is being overcome with the city of God even now.

Every time a soul says, "Jesus, forgive me and take me as your own," a bright new flower emerges in this gray city of man. Every child taught to love the Savior becomes a magnificent display of God's bright red heart and is like a summer-red geranium standing happily in the midst of a foreboding cold gray background. Every act of kindness in Jesus' name, every moment of quiet submission to the will of God, every prayer for the persecuted saint, every cry for a soul to be saved is a new flower blossoming up in this overcast city.

As beautiful as this sight is, one day it will be even more glorious, for this world will be renewed. Eden will be restored. That is where all of our lives are moving this very day. You are a beautiful sight, dear child of God, and your faith and our churches beautify this

1. Romans 5:20.

world. One day the background itself will match the ornaments. Misty darkness will be over. The contrasts of good and evil, light and dark, righteous beauty and sinful ugliness will be changed into singular, unimpaired, undiluted, sheer beauty. Because the Lamb is its lamp, the City of God will finally overtake the city of man. On that day, the skies and the buildings and the hearts of all will finally, for all time, be gloriously, happily, and mercifully transformed.

Our Lord's cross was the beginning. The open tomb was the first day of beauty that will lead to this final era of beauty. Today, that transformation is one day closer. Through your faith, your life being lived out with the beauty of God's grace amidst the sometimes-difficult backdrop of pain and sorrow, a new day is being born. See, it is already coming as your lips form a simple prayer to Jesus Christ from your sickbed! Behold, the snapdragons are blooming though the heartache wilts all things around you!

Therefore we can laugh and smile and take in the beauty we see in granite gray Aberdeen. The City of God is growing, from the inside out, in the city of man. Through the mist, the sea gull's mourning is not what we thought at all—for she is longing for a new day that is on its way.

12

THE CASE OF THE
FRAUDULENT DOUGHNUT

*On Naming Our Sins
and Coming Clean in Christ*

*If we say we have no sin, we deceive ourselves,
and the truth is not in us. —1 John 1:8*

scanned the headlines: "Blair Surprise Visit to
Iraq," "Rivals in Debate Take Aim at Dean," "Rover
Unfurls, Opening New Stage in Exploring Mars,"
"LSU Claims National Title," and some little story
about Brittany's marriage and annulment.

Then I saw it: "The Quest to Deliver the Diet Doughnut." Drawn by my own yearnings for those incredible
little round confections concocted from fried dough

and sugar, I read on. In my first amusement of the day, we learned that a Mr. Robert Ligon had lied about his doughnut. This businessman had marketed his doughnuts as low fat, and he was found to be a fraud. In fact, he had purchased the doughnuts from another business and simply stuck a low fat label on them. He claimed he was innocent, but the court found him guilty of doughnut fraud in the first degree. What did this diabolical doughnut fiend get for his sham? He got a free stay in prison—done in by a doughnut.

I laughed. Then I thought of how even believers seek to cloak their sins by calling them "personality flaws," "little idiosyncrasies," or other euphemisms. Rather than hating our sins, we embrace them as a part of our character that cannot and should not change. Our little lies, our half truths, our gluttonies, our put-downs, our acidic, private comments about those in leadership, our nasty, nose-in-the-air, condescending attitudes toward the poor or the uneducated, the little glances we steal to satisfy our sensual lusts, the proud look, the prideful eye—these are sins, and according to the law of God, they deserve punishment. Every day "Mr. Ligons" come to me, done in by a little flirting, a little padding of the expense account, a little boasting, a little loafing, a little white lie. Switching the label— that's all it is.

Little sins can make big headlines. The biggest story in our lives is that we are sinners. It may be a doughnut caper or it may be adultery or murder, but it is sin. The reason that Christ came was to expose sin and call us to come clean and see our need for his salvation: "**And when he comes, he will convict the world concerning sin and righteousness and judgment**" (John 16:8).

When we speak of the matter of sin and the fall of man, we are dealing with what people like least about Christianity. They don't like the truth-in-advertising label that says man is a sinner and can't save himself. Yet the reality of our sin and the need for a Savior is the very heart of our religion. An old Puritan, Joseph C. Philpot (1802–1869), said, "Man's religion is to build up the creature. God's religion is to throw the creature down in the dust of self-abasement, and to glorify Christ." When we hide the fact of sin and its consequences before a holy God, we distort the Bible, dilute the cross, and deface the very idea of God.

We speak of justification because, without Christ, we are unjust before God. We speak of the cross because we are in sin and someone has to pay for that sin. Christ did so by being cursed on a cross by God his Father for the sins of his people. We speak of salvation because we need to be saved from eternal punishment. We speak of sanctification, of increasingly hating our sin and increasingly being conformed to God's will for our lives, because by nature we are not holy. The only way to sanctification is through the appointed means of grace: Word, sacrament, and prayer. In his old age John Newton said, "My memory is nearly gone, but I remember two things—that I am a great sinner, and that Christ is a great Savior." Perhaps that is the biggest headline.

We are great sinners and Jesus Christ is a great Savior—that is our truth-in-advertising label. Doughnuts, anyone?

13

THE DEATH OF A TV CRITIC

*For it is a land of images, and they are mad
over idols. —Jeremiah 50:38*

On Sunday, October 5, 2003, Neil Postman died of lung cancer at age 72. Now that may not mean much to you. Indeed, if you get most of your news from television outlets, you may not hear much about it because Postman was an ardent critic of television. I quote from the *New York Times* obituary:

> His career was a long-distance joust with what he saw as the polluting effects of television. Postman's core message was that an immersion in a media environment shaped children's lives to their detriment, and society's.
>
> He drew national attention with *The Disappearance of Childhood* (1982), in which he asserted that

71

TV combined what should be the separate worlds of children and adults. It did so, he contended, by steeping the minds of children in vast amounts of information once reserved for their elders and subjecting them to all the desires and conflicts of the adult world. Postman was particularly offended by the presentation of TV news with all the trappings of entertainment programming, including theme music and "talking hairdos." Only in the printed word, he said, could complicated truths be rationally conveyed.[1]

In his many other books—and I commend them all to you, especially *Amusing Ourselves to Death: Public Discourse in the Age of Show Business* (1985), *Technopoly: The Surrender of Culture to Technology* (1993), and *Building a Bridge to the Eighteenth Century* (1999)— this brusque Jewish professor wrapped his formidable intellect and research around the idea that truth had been distorted, if not hijacked, by image. His yeoman-like research, his brilliant analysis, and his clever pen dealt with subjects such as how the television age is changing the way churches worship, how advertising aimed at children is robbing them of childhood, and how Westerners are becoming more technologically advanced and yet more illiterate than their parents. His work found a large audience with Bible-believing evangelicals, and I hope that out of the many occasions he could have heard the gospel, he finally received Christ before his death. I do not know.

1. Wolfgang Saxon, "Neil Postman, 72, Mass Media Critic, Dies," *New York Times*, October 9, 2003. Available online at http://www.nytimes.com/2003/10/09/obituaries/09POST.html?ex=1381032000&en=b8599f34 3b896c35&ei=5007&partner=USERLAND.

Postman is a loss, but others are carrying on his critical message. Marva Dawn, a committed Christian and a professor at Regent College, Vancouver, is one person taking over where Postman left off and applying his thoughts to the church in our time. The questions she is asking are important ones that need to be addressed. In her book *Reaching Out without Dumbing Down*, Marva Dawn describes her experience at the 1987 Vancouver World's Fair, where the Christian pavilion's presentation utilized glitzy double-reversed photography and flashing lasers. She writes,

> When I tried to explain my qualms about the production to an attendant who had asked me how I liked their "show," she protested that it had saved many people. I asked, "Saved by what kind of Christ?"[2]

Dawn follows this by writing the following:

> If people are saved by a spectacular Christ, will they find him in the fumbling of their own devotional life or in the humble services of local parishes where pastors and organists make mistakes? Will a glitzy portrayal of Christ nurture in new believers his character of willing suffering and sacrificial obedience? Will it create an awareness of the idolatries of our age and lead to repentance? And does a flashy, hard-rock sound track bring people to a Christ who calls us away from the world's superficiality to deeper reflection and meditation?[3]

2. Marva Dawn, *Reaching Out without Dumbing Down* (Grand Rapids, MI: Wm. B. Eerdmans Co., 1995).
3. Ibid.

Is the wisdom and insight of people like Postman and Dawn calling us to smash our televisions and do away with the best worship reforms that have come about in the last twenty years? No, I don't think so. But in many ways our world has become, like that of the ancient people of God, a "land of images." The images appear on television, on billboards, in magazines, in video games, in music videos, and even in church. I'm not knocking any of these things, but the warnings of Postman and Dawn are worth listening to, for they reflect the message of God's Word.

"In the beginning was the Word, and the Word was with God, and the Word was God. . . . And the Word became flesh and dwelt among us, and we have seen his glory, glory as of the only Son from the Father, full of grace and truth" (John 1:1,14).

14

IRENE DUNNE,
NEIL POSTMAN,
AND THE RIGHT USE
OF ENTERTAINMENT

*W*hen the late, great Neil Postman (1931–2003) wrote *Amusing Ourselves to Death* (1985), he spoke of a generation that we all know too well. Our money, our priorities, our talk, our time, and thus our lives, are consumed with Britney's regrettable public emotional problems, the Super Bowl commercials that will soon be upon us, and Tom Cruise's controversial scientology. But by living through the tragedy and comedy of others' lives, we may forfeit our own lives.

Irene Dunne knew that. And she did not forfeit her life. Irene Dunne (1898–1990) has been called the greatest actress to never win the Academy Award. I have seen that quote several times by those speaking of her, and I certainly share that opinion. I challenge you to watch Irene Dunne in *My Favorite Wife*, or *The Awful Truth*, or the moving *Penny Serenade*, and show me a more talented actress-singer-comedienne. Watch *I Remember Mama*, but watch it with a handkerchief nearby. Her performance in that one movie far surpasses much of what I see today in the work of Oscar-toting actresses. She was strikingly beautiful and enormously gifted for drama, musicals, or comedy (an art at which I think she was one of the best and most underrated).

I still think no one could really keep up with the presence of Carey Grant like Irene Dunne. Indeed, it could be argued that at times Carey Grant seemed to be trying to keep up with Irene Dunne! But it was never competitive for her. That was always clear. She proved with her life that she was not bridled by ambition. Maybe she transcended becoming just another pretty starlet because, in her early days, she was never a chorus girl. She used to talk about that. She came to theater and acted and didn't have to take the chorus line route or the director's private office route. She was better than they were. She knew herself. She didn't need to sell her life to share her gifts.

She was the daughter of a Louisville riverboat man, a U.S. steamboat inspector. He greatly influenced her and shaped her self-confidence and identity. Some have said that her humor came through her father. Maybe the rides up and down the river on the steamboat while hearing her father's stories shaped her humor. After her father's death (there came her pathos), she moved to Madison, Indiana.

Like so many of our greatest, Irene Dunne was a Midwestern actor in the same vein as Jimmy Stewart and Ronald Reagan. Plain, clear, unpretentious, and tethered to home, not to an allusive dream. It was in Indiana, under the mentorship of her concert-piano-teacher mother, that she grew in her calling. Growing up, her home was filled with music, and it rubbed off on this young lady. She studied voice. She had a captivating operetta singing voice that was happily featured in several of her films. She tried out for but didn't make the Met. We are all thankful for that, for one closed door led to other open doors in theater, and eventually movies.

Here is what really grabs me: Irene Dunne just stopped. She acted, but then she stopped. She married a dentist, Dr. Francis Griffin, and stayed married to him until he preceded her in death. They adopted one child, Mary Frances, who became their little girl in 1938, from the New York Foundling Hospital, run by the Sisters of Charity of New York. She stopped acting to focus on being a mother and a wife. As she put it, "I drifted into acting and drifted out. Acting is not everything. Living is."

She spent the remaining years of her life dedicating much to the Roman Catholic Church and to Republican causes. In 1985 she was awarded the Kennedy Honors by Ronald Reagan, an old friend. This Hollywood beauty was never a Hollywood bimbo. She was a smart, professional actress who gave us much in her gifts. But she didn't live for us. She lived, according to her own demonstrated life, for God and for others. Her own trust helped many in the Roman Catholic communities. Although she could have kept going, kept amusing us all, she just retired from acting to "living." She is the antidote to "amusing ourselves to death." We need more like her.

Neil Postman once wrote, "I don't think any of us can do much about the rapid growth of new technology. However, it is possible for us to learn how to control our own uses of technology."[1] Irene Dunne taught us how to do that. With sparkling eyes, a mischievous grin, and a Jimmy-Stewart Midwestern delivery, she sang and acted and laughed her way into American film history. Then she controlled her own destiny. She put down the remote. She put up the games. She lived.

In between your own living check out one of the most talented actresses in American film in *The Awful Truth* (1937), *Love Affair* (1939), *My Favorite Wife* (1940), *Penny Serenade* (1941), and *I Remember Mama* (1948). Enjoy. Even be amused.

---

1. Neil Postman in answer to a question by Paige MacLean in an online forum, "Neil Postman Ponders High Tech," January 17, 1996, *PBS*, http://www.pbs.org/newshour/forum/january96/postman_1-17.html.

15

THE EMBALMING OF SIN

*I write to you, dear children, because your
sins have been forgiven on account of his
name. —1 John 2:12, NIV*

The *Atlantic Monthly* had an interesting article
recently about the men in Russia who embalmed
Lenin. As you probably know, the founder of one
of the most brutal systems in world history, though
dead, remained viewable by millions through the art
of embalming and technological innovations that preserved the dead tyrant's body under glass. The article
said that those men not only made a living by regulat-
ing the body of Lenin (who even gained a little weight
during one period of his death), but also by seeking to
preserve the corpses of several other atrocious former
dictators. With the fall of Communism, the market for

embalming diabolical despots and dastardly dictators got dead cold.

As I read the article I thought of how we as forgiven children of God, transformed by his grace and power, sometimes, to our own horror, embalm our old sins, our old nature, and put the old man on display. We like to visit the old dead carcass every now and then. We stand and gaze upon this old man and again, to our own hurt, think about him. In this way, though dead, he still holds a sort of sway over us—like a stiffened Lenin.

I spend no small amount of time speaking with people who are Christians but are still plagued by the sight of their old sin. Like the morbid Russian morticians who preserved a dead despot, they preserve their sins, live in their old pain, maintain the hurt and the pain that an old sin brought. New life is inhibited because an old carcass is still on display in their hearts and minds.

But Jesus Christ has abolished our sin. As far as the east is from the west, our sins are done away with and they are no more. Our sins were put on Jesus at the cross. Much like the masses overthrew Communism, Hebrews reminds us to overthrow our morbid preoccupation with old sins and to set ourselves free from the Lenin-under-glass experiences that haunt us. In Hebrews, Jesus is presented as the High Priest who atones for sin once and for all.

> "This is the covenant I will make with them
>   after that time, says the Lord.
> I will put my laws in their hearts,
>   and I will write them on their minds."

Then he adds:

> "Their sins and lawless acts
>   I will remember no more."

And where these have been forgiven, there is no longer any sacrifice for sin. (Hebrews 10:16–18, NIV)

Little lamb of God, your sins are forgiven. They have been put on Jesus. The sooner you come to understand this, the freer you will be, the happier you will be, and the more you will begin to embrace the new life that God has given you. You are not meant to keep those old sins under glass, for they are now and forever under the blood.

16

A DELAYED SALVATION

Who are kept by the power of God through
faith for salvation ready to be revealed in the
last time. —1 Peter 1:5

Not long ago, a friend of mine came by to talk about salvation. Those who characterize themselves as unbelievers may find this strange, but Christians talk about such things. We talk about it because since we have been awakened by God's Holy Spirit and have been made aware of our sins, his salvation, and the new life he has given us, nothing is more important. This is not obsession or undue introspection; it is our hope, our life. Such thinking is, to me, more real, more authentic, than not thinking about it.

At any rate, my friend wept as he talked about his salvation, because after years of serving the Lord, the pain of his past seemed to be mitigating the promised joy of the Lord. A complicated narrative looms over his life like a sinister low-depression storm that won't budge. It is a story of parental neglect that led to insecurity and a depression of the soul. This man did not lack in biblical understanding, in sitting under the preaching of God's Word, or in loving or serving others. He is a model, in fact, to this often-faltering preacher. But he told me of a life spent in pleading for Christ to take away the pain. This man—a Christian leader for most of his life—has spent his secret moments in prayer, asking God to fill his spirit with an illusive joy. He sat before me, his head in his hands, wanting to know what was wrong with him. "Why can't I know the joy that others know?"

Sin can poison the fruit of joy. Undisciplined living can stunt the growth of any potential buds. But I saw none of that. So what do you do when you are doing all of the "right stuff" and still no living water is gushing out of your heart? It is enough to make you doubt your salvation. It is enough to drive you to your knees day in and day out, seeking and searching for God in the midst of all his promises.

What I told him that day I want to tell you, because I believe that what he went through is what many professing believers go through. If you are a distant follower of the Lord, maybe a bit cynical about the whole evangelical Christian thing, then read on. I want to explode some myths about the abundant life, and I also want to bring the hope of God's grace to the rest of us who sometimes pretend that we have it all together but don't. These thoughts are intended to be—like new radiation treatments for cancer patients—small but potent well-placed arsenals against the pseudo-perfect evangelical Christian family, to bring life and healing and hope.

A great life verse for those who, like my friend, struggle with depression and with lingering heartaches and painful memories would be 1 Peter 1:5: "Who are kept by the power of God through faith for salvation ready to be revealed in the last time" (NKJV). The context of this verse is the promise of a "living hope through the resurrection of Jesus Christ from the dead, to an inheritance incorruptible and undefiled and that does not fade away, reserved in heaven" for God's people (1 Peter 1:3–4, NKJV).

Just another verse to heap guilt on the lonely pretender who can't make sense of God's grace in the midst of his or her depression? I don't think so. In fact, I would say that the "happy verses" are never intended to create a press release version of a disciple, and any attempt to create one distorts God's intention for our lives. I believe this is something I call "delayed salvation."

What is delayed salvation? When Peter wrote from "Babylon" (his own place of hardship, likely Rome) and spoke of "being kept by the power of God through faith for salvation ready to be revealed in the last time," he was not denying the work of conversion (1 Peter 5:13). He was affirming the doctrine of the perseverance of the saints—what God starts, God completes (Philippians 1:6). He was also saying that it is not over. He was telling bewildered Christian refugees (1 Peter 1:1) who were suffering the common but extraordinary insults, slanders, isolations, deprivations, and beatings that there is another salvation, a final salvation, a consummation of all God intends. The promises of God's blessings are held in faith through trials and suffering to the ultimate day of salvation.

This does not mean that there is an absence of God in the midst of suffering. Just the opposite. God is there, but he is silent. I do not know why, you do not know why, but we do know we are being kept, preserved by him for a "salvation ready to be revealed."

Back to my friend and back to my pastoral concern for him and others like him. I told my friend that the very sufferings, the very longings in his heart, the unrequited pain, the years and years (he is in his seventies) of seeking the Lord, have unfathomable meaning and purpose. I cannot say why, but I know that the thing that has brought him pain has been the thing that has brought him to the Lord. Indeed, it is the very longing for God in the midst of his heartache that keeps him seeking the Lord. The cross of Jesus Christ is the answer, as usual. The place of torment and shame, the unspeakable place of cosmic sorrow where creature murders creator—a God-ordained deicide—has become the place of salvation and hope.

For my friend, and maybe for you, the cross means that our depressions may be healed by God in our lives on earth, and the heartaches etching the lining of our souls may receive sacred filling—but maybe not. Maybe our damaged emotions and our deep longings will be the things that keep us close to the Lord. "Does a good father ignore his frail child?" I asked my suffering friend. "No," he said. "He loves him—maybe even more." That was a breakthrough. "Yes! Now we are on to something!" I put my hand on his shoulder.

I want—now, at this very point—to reach out to you. Yes, the Father loves you who suffer your whole life. I speak to young parents with children who have Down syndrome. I speak to middle-aged women who suffered abuse as little girls. I speak to children orphaned and raised in a series of foster homes. I speak to doctors who overachieve because they are trying to prove something to a father who never cared. I speak to pastors who are loading up their calendars and calling it "ministry" to compensate for the rejection by the elder in their first charge. I speak to the older couple who longed for children but were given none. I speak to the single woman about to go to yet another wedding. I speak to my own heart.

God loves his frail children, but here is the beauty of Peter's promise of a delayed salvation: the unrestricted joy flowing through your life which you have only dreamed of, the final answer you have craved all of your life, the deep sense of belonging you have always wanted, the end to the cycle of dreams that you have feared all of your life, the release of the soul that you felt was bound up in your complicated life for so many years, will all receive a final salvation on the last day. The joy will be all the more sweet on that day. Pie in the sky, you say? No. Pleasure in the Presence, says Peter.

I did not want to minimize the longing heart of my friend, and I do not want to minimize the sufferings of those who read this. I do want you to know that while God's Word does not reveal all of the reasons for this delayed salvation, it is certain that, as in the case of a delayed healing of Lazarus, God delays a salvation, a healing, a resolution, an answer, a fulfillment, for his own glory and for our own good. So we are back to faith—a faith in suffering and a faith in winter.

My friend and I prayed. I prayed for removal of the thorn in his flesh, and we left the disposition of this matter with a wise and loving God who answers prayer. We knew that he would be healed, we knew joy would come in the morning, but we also knew that the thing haunting him was giving him a poor-in-spirit quality to life that kept bringing him back again and again to the Good Shepherd. We did not celebrate the pain; we trusted the plan. We did not desire more of it, but more of God in it if it was to remain. We affirmed that no matter what, my friend was in the loving grip of the grace of Jesus. We believed together for a salvation, even a salvation that may be "revealed in the last time." I saw his smile that said to me, "It's not over, is it?"

No, the pain is likely not over. But the grace of God is implanted in your newborn soul, slowly releasing the infinitely amazing resurrection power of Jesus Christ directly onto the cancer cell on your soul. You will be healed—soon. "Who are kept by the power of God through faith for salvation ready to be revealed in the last time" (1 Peter 1:5, NKJV).

17

BISCUITS, BACON GREASE, GETTING LOST, AND THE VOICE THAT LEADS ME HOME

*I*n a faraway place called "childhood" in South Louisiana, I loved to go off into the woods and "get lost." When I think back on it, it seems like it was always on a chilly fall morning that I would go on a journey, not sure where I would end up—and that was the best part of it all! The journey was the fun, and the bends and turns in the path I took led me to creeks here and mud holes there, to beehives on one path and majestic old beechnuts with bushy-tailed squirrels on another path.

To take such a journey, I needed food. So Aunt Eva, who always seemed to have bacon and biscuits on the stove, would fix me a little brown bag to take along.

The thing I loved to get in that little bag was a biscuit dabbed in bacon grease. Now, before you throw your Lipitor bottle at me, it was really delicious, and I didn't do it all the time—just sometimes. And it wasn't a whole blob of bacon grease, just a little, with crumbles of the bacon in it. If there were actual bacon strips on the biscuit, then all the better.

What wonderful times they were! As I made my way deep into the chilly woods to explore the unknown, I was happy that I had that little brown bag of biscuits and bacon grease in my pocket, which reminded me that I had food for the journey. They also reminded me of the one who had prepared it. Sometimes I would be gone all day.

On one journey I didn't just pretend to get lost; I really got lost. Aunt Eva came searching. I heard her as she called, and the sound of her voice led me out of the woods. The little brown bag sustained me on the journey; her voice led me home.

In Exodus, God was about to lead his children on the journey of a lifetime. However, before they left, they would come to know his power. They would see something even more radical than a biscuit dipped in bacon grease. They would see blood smeared on a doorpost. They would remember it through eating a meal that would tell and re-tell the story of salvation, liberation, and divine protection.

That meal is fulfilled in the Lord's Supper and is more than a meal and a ceremony. It is a "little brown bag" for sojourners on their way. The road will turn, the pathways will bring surprises, but they will not forget that there is one who loves them and will feed them along the way.

Those pathways I followed in childhood are probably covered over with wild ivy or washed away with decades of seasons come and gone. The beehives are, no doubt, all abandoned; the beechnut might have fallen. The distance between those lost childhood pathways and the little brown bag I carried off in the woods is getting greater and greater. Aunt Eva has finished her journey and is at home with the Lord.

I don't get to wander off in the woods as often as I would like, and I certainly don't eat biscuits and bacon grease anymore. But I am on a journey, and I do have food. The food for my journey is the body and the blood of a Lamb. That Lamb is Jesus. Each day as I feed on him by faith through prayer and his Word, I am reminded that my salvation was not my doing. It is God's love poured out for me. I am saved, I am secure, and I can make the journey because of him— all because of him, only because of him. If I get lost along the way, he will be there, I will hear his voice, and he will lead me all the way home.

18

DA-DEEE!

Because you are sons, God sent the Spirit of his Son into our hearts, the Spirit who calls out, "Abba, Father." So you are no longer a slave, but a son; and since you are a son, God has made you also an heir. —Galatians 4:6–7, NIV

It was Father's Day. Just a few rows from the front of the church sat a young couple with their five-year-old son, listening to the message on fatherhood. Clearly their little tike was not impressed with the sermon, and as everyone around him could see, a wiggle worm had gotten ahold of him. The more mom and dad tried to still him, the more he wiggled, until finally the determined wiggling progressed to a defiant wrestling! The little fellow was just plain fed up with the whole thing and started crying and complaining.

Probably that dad was thinking, *It's Father's Day, and everyone here is looking at me and they can see that I am completely out of control as a dad!*

Finally, the dad grabbed his boy in his arms and made his way across the legs and laps of a whole pew full of worshippers before breaking free into the aisle. Just as he did, that little boy screamed at the top of his lungs, "Da-deeeeeeee!" The sermon stopped. Heads turned. The mother froze and slid down in the pew. On that Father's Day, that little guy took center stage. The father put it into overdrive and made it down the aisle to the back door. As the cry of the child became fainter and the congregation settled down again, the pastor resumed his message.

Of course, the dad was more upset and embarrassed than anyone else. I always say that those are just the sounds of life, and I love them. I would rather have crying kids in the congregation than no kids at all.

After the service, an older gentleman greeted the minister. "Pastor," he said, "that was the greatest sermon ever." Before the minister could offer a sincere thank you, the man went on. "That little boy screaming 'Da-deee'—that's the sermon that hit me! That cry of 'Da-deee' pierced my heart. I used to be a dad of a little boy just like that, and that cry made me think about how much my son needed me. I wish I had done more as a dad. I mean . . . " he caught himself about to cry.

The pastor could see the familiar regret taking hold, and he reached out to put his hand on the man's shoulder. Suddenly, the gentleman looked up again. "You know what, Preacher? My boy is thirty-five years old now, and he still needs me. I am going to call him right now and tell him how much I love him." On that day a squirming little five-year-old preacher delivered a sermon that changed a man's life.

Every now and then when I hear a child cry "Da-deee!" I turn and look, even when I know that neither John Michael nor any of our grown children are around. I always want to answer that cry. I pray I am always there as a father to meet the needs of my children. As a boy who grew up without a father, I used to cry "Da-deee!" in the secret places of my heart. Yes, that was a sorrow. But that cry, that longing for a father, was a sorrow that Christ sanctified and used to draw me to himself.

Many such cries are going out today, and for each one of them, the heavenly Father is there. In fact, that longing for daddy was placed there by the Lord. The longing for a father is the God-ordained desire for intimacy with Abba, who loved us so much he sent his only Son. One day, God's Son cried out to his Father from a sin-laden cross, and his Father could not answer. That day the love God had for you stilled his voice to his own Son. But through the love of a Father and the sacrifice of a Son, you and I may cry out, "Abba," and he will answer, "I am here."

19

ON THE DEATH OF CZESLAW MILOSZ AND THE HOPE OF ALL EXILES

*By faith he went to live in the land of
promise, as in a foreign land, living in tents
with Isaac and Jacob, heirs with him of the
same promise. —Hebrews 11:9*

There were three things I wanted to do that morning: drink coffee, read the *London Times*, and share Christ with a Polish fellow I met at Starbucks.

I made my way down the cobblestone streets of old Aberdeen, under the tolling bell of St. Nicholas Church, through the drifting North Sea mist, and past the grim expressions of black-clad students and laughing children (who have not yet learned to still their God-given joy for life with the nihilistic notions of post-Christian

Britain). I popped into the little newspaper store on King Street, where pornographic magazines were routinely stacked next to children's crossword puzzle books and cheap Scottish tourist stuff, and located the *London Times*. Heading now to the nearest Starbucks, next to the St. Nicholas churchyard, I paid for a Grande Guatemala Antigua and a savory cheese croissant and sat down outside.

Amidst the seagulls' crusty white deposits on a green, wobbly, wrought-iron patio table, I began to peruse the world according to the *Times*. It was then, as I burned my top lip on the steaming coffee and thumbed past the latest blow by blow of Tony and Cheri Blair's holiday itinerary, the most recent Olympic scandals, the latest British soldier killed in Iraq, and the Home Secretary's affair with a married woman, that I located that part of the *Times* called "The Register." There, where famous men and women are eulogized on the most famous obituary page in the world, all of the images and sounds of the morning—the ubiquitous American coffee chain, the ugly site of pornography mixed with children's books, the sad faces, the bells of St. Nicholas—converged as I looked upon the headline for Monday, August 16, 2004: "Czeslaw Milosz: Nobel-prize-winning Polish poet and critic of communism, who, for all his travels, never mentally left the place of his birth." I remembered and I longed for home.

Though I am frequently disturbed by the poetry of Milosz, I still admire and enjoy it. He is, in my opinion, a poet for our time. Dr. Jill Baumgaertner, poetry editor and dean of humanities and theological studies at Wheaton College, calls the Nobel Prize-winning poet "A prophet who . . . awakens in us the awareness that because of the horrors of our times and the vaporization of meaning, the human heart hungers for something that pushes us beyond both the horrible and the trivial."[1]

Born a Pole in Russia in 1911, Milosz was of a generation born into an epic: the Russian revolution and the rise of Communism with its seduction, its lies, its utter brutality and inhumanity. He escaped the Soviet chains over Poland and eventually made his way to Paris before settling in California for most of his adult years. A Catholic, Milosz grew in faith through the years. I think the *Times* was right when it noted, "he was a man who only increased in his strength as he left retirement age farther and farther behind him." His faith and vision of Jesus Christ was central to his writings and to the decisive moments of his life. To miss that is to miss the essence of the man. Milosz's faith was formed not only in an orthodox belief in the divine nature of our Lord, but also in an equally orthodox belief in Christ's humanity. But for Milosz, Christ's humanity was not just an article of faith; it was also a necessity for living—at least for living his own life in the twentieth century.

For most of his life the poet Czeslaw Milosz was a stranger in a strange land, desperately needing to know that God had come down to identify with him in the places of his life and that, on the cross, Jesus was not only God, but also man. He believed in a Savior who willingly exiled himself from heaven in order to redeem men who were exiled from their home with God. For

1. "Reference Publications," *bnet* (CBS Interactive, Inc., 2009), Czeslaw Milosz, "Lecture V" (Christian Century, 2002), http://www.findarticles.com/p/articles/mi_m1058/is_26_119/ai_96195178.

all of his life, through the eye-opening reality of the horror of man's sinful possibilities (as demonstrated in the regicide of the Czar and his family and the millions of Christians killed by Lenin and Stalin) and the acute awareness of his own propensity for sin, Milosz knew that the divine and human Christ was there. His theology is not stated like a systematic textbook, but rather sifted and tested in the wilderness of exile, expressed through painful introspection, and shared, mercifully and thankfully, with other exiles in some of the most human verses I have ever read. He saw his poetry as a gift of God and somehow knew that his poetry was prophecy—not in a predictive way, but in an unmasking of the truth of man and the truth of God. He struggled with his calling in "The Garden of Earthly Delights" and wrote, "My Lord, I loved strawberry jam . . . also well-chilled vodka, herring in olive oil, scents, of cinnamon, of cloves. So what kind of prophet am I? Why should the spirit have visited such a man? Many others were justly called, and trustworthy. Who would have trusted me?"

But he always seemed to know the answer. God has placed the treasure of the gospel in earthen vessels. And so he would also write in "Lecture V," about the mystery of the kingdom that has come and the evil that remains, "'Christ has risen.' Whoever believes that should not behave as we do."[2]

The wandering poet, exiled from his home, finally returned. In the spring of 1989, exactly fifty years after he left, Milosz did what American Thomas Wolfe said could never happen. He went home again. Now gray, with lines marking so many passages, so many experi-

2. Ibid.

ences, the old poet faced his past and came to grips, for all of us, with a devastating century. In his collection of poems *Facing the River*, the banks of the river of the Issa Valley in modern Lithuania became the place where Milosz reflected on his life, our lives, and our century. He thought of empires rising and empires crumbling; of savored moments kept in his heart forever; and wasted, sinful, and silly times that he regretted. And through it all, there was Christ. In the midst of it all there was the cross. And somehow there was still the church.

I put down the paper and thought of how, for this moment, I was an exile. Though happily on vacation, I was not at home with those seagulls. The North Sea mist was not mine. The souls around me were in need of Christ, but there was a flock of saints back in Chattanooga of which I was pastor. There was a nation I loved that was sliding to Gomorrah. At that moment I wanted so much to be a prophet in Babylon, with the captives in Babylon, if that is what we have become. I just wanted to go home. I asked Mae and John Michael and they also wanted to go home again. It had been fun. Vacation had been relaxing for us. But our hearts were in another place. We, too, wanted to face the river.

Then I remembered. I had not only wanted to sip coffee and read the *Times*, I had specifically wandered out that morning to that place in order to share Christ with the young Pole I had met at Starbucks. We had talked of many things in the two weeks I had been there. I liked him intuitively, and we had become friends. I wanted to pray with him. Did he know about Milosz's death? I suddenly thought, *Being a Pole, he surely would have known about him.* Milosz's death would be my conversation starter, and then I would ask him to pray with me to receive Christ.

"Where is that young Polish fellow who works here?" I asked the redheaded Scottish Starbucks barista-lass behind the counter.

"I'm sorry. He no longer works here, and he has also moved away. He left suddenly."

Maybe he heard. Maybe he went back, himself—to the River.

I prayed for his soul. I thought about how sacred are the moments when we find other souls on this journey, in this exile. And I asked God to help me be more alert, more brokenhearted, and more willing to identify myself as his disciple quickly and openly and responsibly. And I thanked God that there were others who would. Maybe, as they say, I had planted a seed; someone else would harvest the fruit. I thanked God for the time to read—even Milosz's poems—and for my Polish friend and for being a pastor in Chattanooga. I walked back to our flat. I passed so many people again. Did they know about Christ? Did they once care and now care no more? Were we all exiles? Were they really home if they looked so sad? How did I appear to them? A stranger? Maybe a bit sad myself? I thought as I walked. Soon I was back to the flat.

We needed to pack. It was time for strangers in a foreign land to go home. Thank God that in Jesus Christ we know where home is.

20

THE WISHBONE
OR THE BACKBONE

I recently read Geoffrey Thomas's book *Preaching: The Man, the Message, The Method*. Compiled by this great Welsh pastor from Aberystwyth from a series of lectures at Reformed Theological Seminary, the book contains a stirring message to those of us called to the ministry: we must rely on God alone for our sustenance in our ministry. At one point in his lectures, Thomas begins to lament the sad situation of preachers shying away from their work because of criticism or opposition. He says that at that point in their ministries, many begin to "wish" for another call, "wish" for another place, "wish" for another church, and "wish" for another pastorate. Thomas writes, "What the preacher needs is not a 'wish-bone' but a back-bone!"

Moses, like many preachers today, lamented his own calling at tough times in his ministry, and his frustration actually caused him to sin against God in Numbers 20:10. Moses snorted and grumbled in self-righteous indignation. "Hear now, you rebels; shall *we* [my emphasis] bring water for you out of this rock?" (Numbers 20:10). Last time anyone checked, Moses couldn't bring water out of any rock, but in anger he used the word *we*. *We* cannot do anything like that. Only *he* can give the water out of the rock.

God interrupts this little pity party and declares Moses' response to be a rebellion in itself. And God said, "Because you did not believe in me, to uphold me as holy in the eyes of the people of Israel, therefore you shall not bring this assembly into the land that I have given them" (Numbers 20:12). The people rebelled, and then Moses rebelled. But Moses' rebellion cost him his leadership. Moses forfeited seeing the vision of his ministry realized because the man who was called to call others to faith didn't believe that God would take care of him in the troubles he faced. He had struck the rock and water had come out, but he had taken the glory from God. This was an open attack by a public leader on the holiness of God. In this one instance of disobedience, Moses lost the privilege to lead the people across to the Promised Land.

How many of us are like Moses? Not only preachers, but Christians in many different places of leadership, influence, and potential for testimony can fall victim to our own flesh at such times of adversity. Many of us forfeit ministry when, like Moses, we stop believing that God can handle any rebellion, difficulty, or trial. Preachers, particularly, may not strike rocks and claim divine powers to excise water, but we may be tempted to say, "You didn't do it my way and now look at what you are facing! I could have fixed this had you left it to me, but now look at the mess you are in!" But when leaders join in with the anger or attack of misguided saints or sinners or answer attacks (as painful as they may be) with self-defensive words, they lose their way on the journey. God had taken up for Moses before and he would have again. He promises to be our portion, our stronghold, our defense, and even our very reputation.

O Lord, save me from my weakness in tough times. I want to go all the way in the journey. I want to give God the glory in good times and bad. Don't you? There is no *we*; there is only *he*.

Whatever you are facing, don't sink to the level of the enemy. Rise to the call of the Savior! Remember his grace in calling you. Remember and rejoice! It is better to be God's man or God's woman and face trials and opposition and suffering than to be apart from God and live a life of ease. When I consider this, I want to cry out to God, "Lord, when times get tough, remind me of your love in electing me, of your grace in saving me, of your mercy in making me your ambassador. O Lord, I don't want to pull on the wishbone; I want to put on some backbone!"

21

This Just In: America Finally Slides over the Slippery Slope

(Hmm . . . Is There Something Else On, Honey?)

*I*n conference after conference I hear it. In article after article I read it. "We are now a postmodern society. We are now post-Christian. We need to learn how to minister to these people." And I have parroted their remarks. I have no doubt that the drumbeat of those words has worked its way into my thinking. I think we started on this journey a long, long time ago, and we may now be sitting right in the midst of it.

Now what is generally meant by this analysis in pastoral circles is that in order to reach the postmoderns, we must change our words, update our worship, alter our communication style, and so forth. But in considering the threat to Bible-believing Christianity, I am not so sure that postmodernity is our greatest threat, and I am not convinced that changing the look and feel of the church helps. In fact, I think it likely hurts. It lulls us into thinking that we are really addressing the issue of our generation. I, for one, do not think this is the issue. Let me explain.

I was refreshed recently when I read the words of one of my favorite thinkers of all things cultural. Richard John Neuhaus wrote in *First Things*: "I have frequently cautioned against the propensity of some conservatives, especially Evangelicals, to claim that ours is a post-Christian society. That is, I contend, an easy out from engaging the tasks that are ours in an incorrigibly, confusedly, and conflictedly Christian America."[1]

That is a caution we should carefully consider. While I must agree with David B. Hart (see his article in the March 2004 issue of *The New Criterion*) that America is characterized by a modernity in which "government insinuates itself into the little liberties of the family," America is also characterized by a society that "allows morality to give way to sentimentality." We have become a nation stewing in our own witch's brew of radical moral decisions (like the codification of gay "marriage"). We are unable to differentiate right from wrong and are dangerously blind to the consequences of our wanton behavior.

The greater issue is something else. Many of us just don't care enough to do anything about the world around us. The truth is, like the few radical groups that are making big problems for our troops in Iraq, the

1. http://www.firstthings.com/article/2009/02/the-catholic-reform—41.

number of those wanting same-sex marriage and abortion on demand and those who want to scratch out "In God We Trust" is probably few, and they are, perhaps, vastly outnumbered by Christians, or at least by those influenced by Christian thinking. Manhattan, Seattle, and Los Angeles notwithstanding, there appear to be an amazingly large number of people who think these things are wrong. Maybe they are not sure why these things are wrong, or maybe *wrong* is too strong a word, but they intuitively sense that these things may not be right (perhaps they are living off of the "moral capital" of a previous generation, as Francis Schaeffer used to put it). The greater risk to liberty, the more dangerous sign of national decay, and the biggest challenge for the American church is that for the most part, we who know right from wrong would simply rather watch television. I mean to say that apathy lulls us to sleep like the drone of a National Public Radio announcer. Those of us who are Christians too often watch Fox News, see yet another example of moral decline and say, "Now that's a shame." Then we flip through the channels to catch the rest of the Braves game. We can watch children starving in Africa and bodies being dragged through the streets of a war-torn Iraqi city, and we can (secretly) enjoy a little soft porn commercial, all without leaving the comfort of our living rooms, and all in about ten minutes. Television has desensitized us. Or at the least, it has turned the wide-screen, full color version of the radical, life-changing, God-induced, resurrection-stunned disciple of Jesus into a fuzzy screened, black and white ho-hum version—with the mute button on.

I think this is our greatest danger, my beloved. I am less concerned about coming up with consumer-driven methods to reach unchurched postmoderns than I am about letting unchurched postmoderns see authentic Christianity on display in my own life. But if I am right (I hope I am wrong, for it is refreshingly easier to deal with figuring out how to deal with postmodernity), then we are in danger of God's judgment. For our Lord Jesus had harsh words for the seventh church, Laodicea, in his letters to the churches. He condemned their "lukewarm" works (Revelation 3:16), and I think he condemns mine. I am so infected by the lackadaisical society around me that every word I write stings me. Yet I am not melancholy about the church today, or about my life or yours, for Jesus Christ extends his invitation—not just to the heathen living in Laodicea, but to the Christians living there and here.

"Behold, I stand at the door and knock. If anyone hears my voice and opens the door, I will come in to him and eat with him, and he with me. The one who conquers, I will grant him to sit with me on my throne" (Revelation 3:20–21). It is that glorious invitation and that wondrous promise that gives me hope. I am excited about the church today. I would rather be alive now than at any other time in history.

What to do? Repent. Not just repent the way we often do—by getting all emotional about it now and then flipping to the next channel in our lives—but by coming clean with God. And then plead for a radical grace-swept soul that will bow down gladly to the Christ of all glory. In his power we withstand the sin and get up from the easy chair and fall to our faces in daily, devout prayer for revival. Through a fresh glimpse of his love for our selfish souls, we must lend a hand to a hurting widow, build a house for a poverty-stricken family, and give away our time, talents, and tithes to see the gospel go to the ends of the earth. In all of it, we must call others to examine the life of Jesus. Just know this: if others accept your challenge to examine the person of Jesus, they will begin by examining your own response to him. And that, surely, is the greatest challenge to the church today.

22

WHO WILL STAND
BY THE DOOR?

O ne life lived for Jesus Christ is powerful, and
the names of those whom we lift up as examples flood our minds: Martin Luther and
John Calvin, Peter Marshall and Jim Elliot, Eric Lid-
dell and Billy Graham, Amy Carmichael and Mother
Theresa. We can live for Christ in whatever we do and
in whatever vocation we pursue. We surely repudiate
any unbiblical idea of clericalism, which says that you
can only be holy if you are a clergyman or some other
kind of religious worker. Alternatively, we believe that
the idea of radical egalitarianism is also wrong-headed.
Egalitarianism sees all things alike, blurs all distinc-
tions, obliterates all particularity. In a radical form of
egalitarianism, we could have no pastors or teachers in
the church. We would be either all laymen or all clerics,
depending upon your point of view (there have been

denominations and movements which have claimed this). This also is wrong.

The Bible clearly teaches that Jesus Christ not only calls laborers for his harvest (Matthew 9:37–38), but he also gives gifts to men (Ephesians 4:8). Those gifts were given as Christ called some to be apostles and prophets, both foundational offices no longer necessary in the church. He also calls people to the continuing and ordinary positions of evangelists, pastors, and teachers (Ephesians 4:11). True, if we are Christ's, then we all are equal in value and worth before the Lord and are all "Abraham's offspring, heirs according to promise" (Galatians 3:29). We raise high the Reformed banner of the priesthood of all believers. But we also recognize the biblical truth that some are called to go in the name of the Lord to serve the world and the church by offering the gifts given by the Lord back to him through consecrated full-time service. I have written about this in my book, *Leaving a Career to Follow a Call: A Vocational Guide to the Ordained Ministry*, but I am very happy to report that John Piper has also addressed this in a much greater book, *Don't Waste Your Life!* Amen!

I believe that God has not stopped giving gifts to men and women. I do not believe that the harvest is over. I believe that God still gifts people and that the call of Jesus Christ resounds in the hearts of his people—especially young people today. In the spirit of the missions conferences that so many churches host, I am praying that God will call all of us to service, to share the gospel, and to support with our prayers and finances the work of world missions. I am also praying that God will call some to be pastors and teachers and missionaries.

Recently, I was discussing a favorite poem with one of my own church's members and found out that it was also her husband's favorite poem. It was written by, perhaps, one of the greatest Episcopal ministers in our nation's history, Samuel Shoemaker. The poem is entitled "I Stand by the Door."

> I admire the people who go way in.
> But I wish they would not forget how it was
> Before they got in. Then they would be able to
> help
> The people who have not yet even found the
> door,
> Or the people who want to run away again from
> God.
> You can go in too deeply, and stay in too long,
> And forget the people outside the door.
> As for me, I shall take my old accustomed
> place,
> Near enough to God to hear him, and know he
> is there,
> But not so far from men as not to hear them
> And remember they are there, too.
>
> Where? Outside the door
> Thousands of them. Millions of them.
> But—more important for me—
> One of them, two of them, ten of them,
> Whose hands I am intended to put on the
> latch.
> So I shall stand by the door and wait
> For those who seek it.

I had rather be a door-keeper
So I stand by the door.[1]

Does the Spirit of God still stir the heart of a young man to preach the gospel of grace to a desperate race and to shepherd the flock of God? Are there any more Samuel Shoemakers or Peter Marshalls or Jim Elliots or Russell Hightowers? Does God still move upon the hearts of young ladies to give their lives away to Jesus Christ and to see the "thousands of them, millions of them" or "one of them, two of them, ten of them" in need of Christ? Are there any more Amy Carmichaels?

We know the answer. But answer this in your own heart: how will you stand by the door?

As David said before he went out to fight Goliath, "Is there not a cause?" May the cross of Christ burn into our hearts the glorious vision of our Savior's love for humanity. May all of us rise to say, "I will stand by the door!" And may many more young men and women rise to give their lives away to a cause that is greater than themselves.

1. The Jaywalker Site, 2008, http://www.thejaywalker.com/pages/shoemaker.html.

23

HOLLYHOCKS, OUTHOUSES, AND VBS

*I*t is amazing the power that a hollyhock had on me one morning. As I went out to get the newspaper, I already had the weight of the world pressing down on me. I was walking, I was breathing, I was thinking, but because of my preoccupation with rescuing the earth from eternal destruction and other similar issues, I was not really living. Or really praying for that matter. Then came one brilliant moment when God disclosed himself to me. It happened as I bent down to get the paper.

As I stretched and grunted to pick up the paper on the curb of my driveway, my eye caught sight of a single hollyhock that I had planted by our mailbox. The hollyhock had bloomed. I had previously noticed one or two yellow flowers coming out, but I had somehow missed the full, glorious blooming that had occurred. There were now yellows and reds and pinks and whites all arranged by God on huge "fig-like" leaves, sitting prettily on a couple of tall, skinny, green stalks.

Now, if you know anything about hollyhocks, you know they are one of those perennials that are advertised in garden magazines as, "old-timey plants just like Grandmother's" or something similar. And it is true. Hollyhocks have a cherished place in the English cottage garden. As our forefathers and mothers came to America, they brought the seeds of those beautiful, spiked, multi-colored staples of the flowerbed with them. It truly is "an old-timey" beauty. I have noticed that there are more of them in Midwestern gardens than Southern ones, but here in Tennessee, I have taken notice of quite a few. The hollyhock is one of those flowers that can evoke memories of childhood at Grandma's house, or Sunday afternoon strolls through a park, or, for me, Vacation Bible School.

There were hollyhocks growing near the outhouse of New Bethlehem Baptist Church, way out in the country near where I grew up. (If you have not had the joy of using an outhouse, particularly an outhouse at a country church with VBS going on, I would love to talk with you about it sometime.) I remember that going to the outhouse was a real pleasure. Yes, that's right; it was a real pleasure. First of all, as a child, I was amazed by a plant that was taller than I was. Hollyhocks can grow to be eight feet tall in the right conditions. Second, they were pretty and reminded me of Miss Dot, our teacher, who I thought was going to be my wife one day. I was seven years old and she was married to a banker, but somehow none of that mattered. Third, bees love hollyhocks, and there was an element of danger in going to the outhouse. It made VBS even more adventuresome.

For that one moment, as I bent down to get the paper and was mesmerized by the hollyhock in full bloom, I remembered the experience of the Holy Spirit moving on my heart at Vacation Bible School. I remember how I got to carry the American flag in the daily processional before we said the Pledge of Allegiance and then the Christian Pledge of Allegiance. I remember cold Kool-Aid on hot, humid days. I remember the crunchy sweetness and floury smoothness of those cookies that came about a million to a pack for 99 cents. I remember waiting for a ride home after it was over at noon. I would slip inside and stand in the pulpit at New Bethlehem Baptist Church and imagine being the preacher. I remember how I felt God was there in that place and that he probably wanted me to do something with his presence. I didn't quite know what he wanted at that time, but I remember his tug at my little heart.

I am thankful for that hollyhock. The Lord used it to remind me about something very important that happens at my own church: "Summer Stomp Camp"—our VBS and music camp—which reaches the church's children as well as children living right down the street from us. Our volunteer teams are sometimes able to place about 300 door hangers on homes. Many of the church members are hard at work preparing for the camp each time it arrives. The gospel of Jesus Christ is presented there. I always pray that our covenant children, who have been reared in the gospel, will be strengthened and challenged to follow the Lord. I pray that children who don't understand God's love in Jesus

Christ will understand for the first time and receive him. And I ask the Lord, who often does his wonderful sovereign work of preparing young, tender hearts for future ministry, to do that here in our church. We don't have hollyhocks growing next to an outhouse. We don't even have an outhouse at First Presbyterian. But I think God will be here anyway. Behind the cookies and the singing and the crafts there is the image of Christ welcoming children and saying, "Let the little ones come unto me."

And when you're at your own church next week, if you see some little child hanging around the sanctuary, maybe "trying out" the pulpit, let him alone. God may be up to something.

24

THE FESTIVITY OF THE POOR

*Hand-Me-Down Pride, Dickens,
and the Reasons We Ought to Be Careful
in Our Ministry to the Poor*

I grew up poor. And when I say that I mean not only that we lived below the poverty level, but that we were poor in spirit. That is, we knew that our condition was one that was dependent, in need, unable to be sustained except by the kindness of others. We were sustained by the state. As conservative, self-reliant Republicans, some of us might not be proud to admit it. But surely, as even the Roosevelt-era Ronald Reagan knew, the state has its place with the poor. Before food stamps there were commodities. And I remember greedily scraping the bottom of the peanut butter can with a spoon and tasting that wonderfully strong peanut fragrance of my favorite commodity that we received, *gratis,* from the U.S. Department of Agriculture.

Each Tuesday a social worker came out to check on the orphan that was given to the widowed childless woman in the woods, my Aunt Eva. This social worker's name was Strauss. Strauss (later I learned she had a first name: Helen) would come out and eat lunch with us. She loved Aunt Eva's vegetables—loaded, as I recall, with lots of pork—and she always, always concluded the meal with cornbread, hot from the skillet, crumbled in a bowl with ice-box chilled buttermilk poured over it. Strauss was the best of government workers. She mixed the state's duty to the poor with her own compassion for the poor. She always brought me a candy bar when she came on Tuesdays, and she also gave me clothing handed down from her grandsons. Her grandsons attended St. Paul's Episcopal School in Hammond, Louisiana. The boys were several years older than me, so when they grew out of their khaki pants and plaid shirts, I got them. When I started to school at Live Oak Elementary School in Watson, Louisiana, I often dressed as if I were going to St. Paul's. I was the poor child attired in the clothes of the affluent.

I thank God for Strauss, for commodity food, for hand-me-downs, for the fellowship of cornbread and buttermilk, and for candy bars on Tuesday. We were poor, but we were not forgotten. We were not inhuman, and we were not statistics. We were also not destined for poverty. My Aunt Eva always told me, "Son, there is nothing for you here. Get a good education and get out. And one day maybe you can take me with you." All of this is to say that there is more to the poor than meets the eye. They are human. And though "the poor you will always have with you," Jesus also came to preach good news to the poor. He said, "Blessed are the poor in spirit."

I have been thinking about how we minister to the poor, because I have been reading G.K. Chesterton's *Charles Dickens, the Last of the Great Men.* In his chapter called "The Alleged Optimism of Dickens," Chesterton shows how Dickens understood the poor in a way that others did not. Most schoolboys know that great social reforms came about as a result of the literary activism of Charles Dickens. His characters and stories revealed a part of London, a poor part that many passed on the way to their stores and their factories, but few saw. Dickens saw them and told us about them. Chesterton disagreed with those who criticized Dickens for making the poor seem happy. We prefer them downcast, misused, forgotten, and condemned to generation after generation of dirty, grimy misunderstanding and forsakenness. Chesterton showed in this chapter that Dickens lifted up the poor by recognizing what he called a "festivity of the poor." I really like that phrase. It admits poverty and all that poverty brings, but it also admits the humanity of the poor, even the laughter and joy that lies in the hearth and hearts of the Cratchits, for instance. I think it is important that we remember that too.

Our churches send out many youth and adult mission trips each year. We go to the cramped and dangerous apartments of the inner city, to the junkyard reservations of the American Indian, to the engine-hanging-on-the-limb landscape of poor white Appalachia, and to the crumbling orphanages of East European cities. We ought to remember as we minister Jesus to the poor that the poor may have something to teach us too. They are human, and they love and laugh and dream and live despite, and sometimes because of, their condition. Somehow when we begin to do this, we come to see life itself in a new way. Chesterton relates what Dickens saw in the lives of the poor.

> He saw all his streets in fantastic perspectives, he saw all his cockney villas as top-heavy and wild, he saw every man's nose twice as big as it was, and every man's eyes like saucers. And this was the basis of his gaiety—the only real basis of any philosophical gaiety. This world is not to be justified as it is justified by the mechanical optimists; it is not that it is orderly and explicable; its merit is that it is wild and utterly unexplained. Its merit is precisely that none of us could have conceived such a thing, that we should have rejected the bare idea of it as miracle and unreason. It is the best of all impossible worlds.

Escaping the utopia bred in unbelief, Dickens saw creation, fall, and redemption all at work in the lives of the poor he sought to help. His assistance, like that of Strauss's in my life, was not an act of pitiful mercy, but of Christlike humanity. He entered their lives and saw them man to man, without atheistic condescension. He celebrated their lives and revealed injustice without removing humanity.

25

FRAGMENTS OF FLOWERS
FOR A LIFE OF MINISTRY

*TO THE CHOIRMASTER: ACCORDING TO THE GITTITH.
A PSALM OF THE SONS OF KORAH. How lovely is
your dwelling place, O LORD of hosts! My soul
longs, yes, faints for the courts of the LORD;
my heart and flesh sing for joy to the living
God. Even the sparrow finds a home, and the
swallow a nest for herself, where she may lay
her young, at your altars, O LORD of hosts, my
King and my God. Blessed are those who dwell
in your house, ever singing your praise! Selah.
—Psalms 84:1–4*

I have been listening to Dan Fogelberg's *The Innocent Age* recently. There is a line in one of his
songs that has stayed in my mind: "Friends we

knew, follow us through all of the days of our lives."
Simple enough. That line makes me think of the collection of lives, like baskets of beautiful flowers, that we
now carry in our hearts. Friends, brothers and sisters
in Christ, who follow us through all of the days of our
lives. I am thinking about them today.

One of the heartaches of pastoral ministry is saying goodbye; but one of the glories of the ministry
is keeping the flock of Jesus in your heart forever. I
have found that I cannot shepherd a flock of Jesus
and then just forget them. Indeed, as you are moved
by the Lord of the harvest from one field to another,
it is like gathering flowers from each field and taking
them with you to the next. Sometimes you pause, and
as you rest, you remember. You remember the hard,
but you also remember the good, the beautiful, the
kind acts of love. And you remember the joys of serving Jesus together.

Recently, the choir of First Presbyterian Church of
Chattanooga commissioned a painting of the stained
glass windows of our church. I used to look at those
windows each week. They were good friends to me
that reminded me, in their grandeur and majesty, of
the transcendence and awe of worshiping the living
God. To see them now, in this beautiful picture, gracing
our wall, allows me to enter again into those sacred
memories of the golden moments of worship in that
beautiful, soaring sanctuary.

In the ministry, it is certain that you will get hurt.
But you will also be blessed beyond anything you
will ever deserve. That is what I have experienced.
And all of this reminds me again, that there is no

higher honor than shepherding the flock of Christ. For at the end of your life, the fragments of flowers, the memory and beauty of all of those souls, will be the essence and joy of your life that you will take to heaven with you.

26

BENIGN NEGLECT
AND QUIET STRENGTH

*But he was wounded for our transgressions; he
was crushed for our iniquities; upon him was
the chastisement that brought us peace, and
with his stripes we are healed. All we like sheep
have gone astray; we have turned—every one—
to his own way; and the LORD has laid on him
the iniquity of us all. He was oppressed, and
he was afflicted, yet he opened not his mouth;
like a lamb that is led to the slaughter, and like
a sheep that before its shearers is silent, so he
opened not his mouth. —Isaiah 53:5–7*

illiam Kristol wrote a syndicated column
recently in which he quoted Pat Moynihan, who was serving on Richard Nixon's

staff. Moynihan, in discussing the clamor to "have a national discussion on race," as we would say, advised the president that what was really needed was a period of "benign neglect." The idea was that more talk, more press conferences, more town hall meetings to talk about race problems would not really help, but would agitate and make things worse. What was needed was quiet, authentic action. I read that and couldn't help but think of an elder in one of our churches who told me, with confessions of his own struggles in this area, "I never got in trouble for what I didn't say!"

I am interested in that one choice phrase "benign neglect" as it relates to pastors and other Christian leaders. There are times to speak up and speak out about things that need to be done at a church, in a person's life, and in the pulpit. There are issues that just seem to demand a pastoral statement. If you are a parent, it is the same way. There are times when your very blood rises within you, and you just know you need to speak to your child. As a military leader, a business leader, a teacher in an elementary school, or a professor in a college, you know this feeling. But I want you to consider the virtue and blessings of selective "benign neglect."

First, let me establish that I am not creating anecdotal ground for my thought. I believe that "benign neglect" is a virtue that God commends. In passage after passage of Scripture we see the wisdom of it. David, sensing that God would both take care of the one who cursed him and take care of David's own sin, trusted the Lord and did not revile Shimei. Instead we read they went on to the Jordan, and there refreshed themselves.

Then Abishai the son of Zeruiah said to the king, "Why should this dead dog curse my lord the king? Let me go over and take off his head." But the king said, "What have I to do with you, you sons of Zeruiah? If he is cursing because the LORD has said to him, 'Curse David,' who then shall say, 'Why have you done so?'" And David said to Abishai and to all his servants, "Behold, my own son seeks my life; how much more now may this Benjaminite! Leave him alone, and let him curse, for the LORD has told him to. It may be that the LORD will look on the wrong done to me, and that the LORD will repay me with good for his cursing today." So David and his men went on the road, while Shimei went along on the hillside opposite him and cursed as he went and threw stones at him and flung dust. And the king, and all the people who were with him, arrived weary at the Jordan. And there he refreshed himself. (2 Samuel 16:9–14)

What gospel beauty is here. The cross of Christ shows that we are sinners, and it also shows the love of Jesus for sinners. It also teaches us that others are sinners. We can leave our insults and our pain with Jesus. We can even entrust the one who hurts us to him. We can come to the cross of Christ, his grace and his forgiving love, and be refreshed in the Jordan-like mercy of God, which quenches the sinner's thirst.

The Indianapolis Colts football coach calls his autobiography *Quiet Strength*. That is a good term for the Old Testament "gospel" that Isaiah prophesied about our Savior: "He was oppressed, and he was afflicted, yet he opened not his mouth" (Isaiah 53:7). Why would this Savior be quiet when afflicted by his own created beings? Because of love. Because of his love for his

Father and his ultimate trust in him, the Son would say to the Father, "Father, forgive them, for they know not what they do." Thus our beloved Jesus astonished the masterfully Machiavellian Pilate:

> But when he was accused by the chief priests and elders, he gave no answer. Then Pilate said to him, "Do you not hear how many things they testify against you?" But he gave him no answer, not even to a single charge, so that the governor was greatly amazed. (Matthew 27:12–14)

Benign neglect. Leaving things alone. Entrusting to God those who curse you. Entrusting yourself and your life to God. Refreshing yourself in his grace, rather than answering in defense.

There are times to speak. And there are times to be quiet. Wisdom from the Word and being steeped in prayerful presence with Jesus Christ is the only way to know which is right. We need more pastors and church leaders of quiet and gentle strength.

27

"YOU GOT TO BELIEVE"

Faith, the KU Jayhawks, and the Christian Life

Those who know me also know that I stay up way too late to watch the NCAA Championship and wake up way too excited, if not tired. Kansas is my adopted home state. My wife and I graduated not from KU, but from two different Kansas colleges that have a strong relationship with KU. We are great fans of the Jayhawks. So, one such morning, I rushed to the online version of the KC Star to see what my favorite sportswriter, Joe Posnanski, had to say. This one line caught me: "Kansas coach Bill Self was on the sideline, and he was shouting to his players, 'You got to believe,' which is as corny a thing as a coach could say, but he could not think of anything else."[1]

1. http://www.kansascity.com/180/story/565754.html (accessed April 8, 2008; site now discontinued).

"You got to believe." With two minutes and nine points down, I have to admit that I might have called it "corny" myself. But I had watched the night before as Mario Chalmers made that amazing three-pointer in the last few seconds to tie it up and send the game into overtime and ultimate victory for his team. "You got to believe."

Some time after that a young man called me. He wanted to talk. And the story he told me was the story of any young person. He is graduating from college. He has had a dream all of his life. And now, with graduation drawing near and others moving on to graduate school or a job, he told me, "Not only does the dream look like it's dead after all of these years, but I have no idea where my next meal will come from in about three months." He then told me his spiritual dilemma: "I know about God's sovereignty. But I don't see it. I am not believing the way I used to. I am in doubt. Did God bring me this far and put this goal on my heart only to frustrate me at the end of this life of preparation? Is God cruel?"

My first thought was that his trial would seem trivial to an older, wiser follower of the Lord. For as we go through life, we learn to trust the providence of God in the dark. We come to understand that today's frustration is tomorrow's testimony. Our heartaches, our trying times of waiting, being suspended like a plane wanting to come down, running out of fuel but getting a "pull up" at the last minute, over and over again, become more familiar, although never easier. The sense of "desertion," as the Puritans called this experience, by this sovereign God we have trusted in is as acute at 80 as it is at 18. But we do come to expect it. We do come to understand that the "dark night of the soul" experiences are not exceptions to the Christian life but norms.

This young man is learning it. And his lack of trust frightened him. That was healthy. This young man was becoming "poor in spirit" and thus more able to receive and steward the gifts of God. I told him as much. I told him that he was embarking upon one of the greatest faith-building times in his life, thus far. But I assured him that this is only the beginning. I also told him that I once thought the old Jewish proverb was a lie when it said, "The man who has never questioned God has never known God." I now consider it thoroughly grounded in biblical truth. And I pointed him to Job, Abraham, and Moses.

Whether it was the apostle John on the Isle of Patmos wondering if the kingdom of God would come, could come, in the presence of the mighty Roman empire, or Simeon in the court of the temple waiting for the Messiah to show up in his lifetime, the Bible is filled with those who wait and wonder. Indeed, God identifies with this young man when in the moment of agony, Jesus prays, "Father, let this cup pass from me, yet not my will but yours be done." Jesus enters into the boiling cauldron of every question about God's goodness and God's sovereignty when on the cross, God in the flesh writhes in pain, becomes a curse on a Gentile cross, undergoes the most incredible "ending" to a dream ever known, and cries out, "My God, my God, why have you forsaken me?"

From the cross to the tomb and from the tomb to the sky, Jesus answers the question. The answer is simply "God." He is in control. Despite every visible, reasonable evidence to the contrary, Jesus rises from the dead and the story does not end. In fact, the apparent aborted end to this Messiah's mission becomes, in the hands of his Father, the point of the whole story. I remember Barth's answer to the question of apologetics: "Jesus is my apologetic." Whatever else we think of Barth's mistakes, that one statement surely stands true. "If Jesus," then me. For he is the firstfruits, St. Paul tells us. The rest of us are following with him. And our faith is not simply a confessional statement, but a confessional statement with flesh on it. The flesh part takes time and years and frustration and heartache and questions and doubt and wonder.

"Now faith is the assurance of things hoped for, the conviction of things not seen" says the writer to the Hebrews (11:1). So I told this young man in the tender years of adulthood what I am still learning at midlife: trusting the Good Shepherd for a good outcome, for tender blades of grass in lush pastures of sunlit uplands, while wandering on the sharp-edged granite cliffs of life, is something that we learn. Faith is a gift, for salvation and for sanctification.

I told the young man to look to some older sheep who have walked this path before, and who walk it with you too, even now, in their own way. Look to the other members of the flock who will tell you that the rocky, wind-swept mountainside is not all there is, and that the Good Shepherd can be trusted to lead us all the way. He is sovereign and thus outside of our control. He sees what we cannot see. Our present predicament in the presence of all of the promises of the Word does not negate his goodness, but proves it. Look to the others. But always, always keep your eyes on Jesus himself. Keep your focus on his life and death and resurrection. We trust God because he is with us. Those souls who have passed through the hard places of life to learn that he can be trusted sing songs. They singer louder and more convincingly than anyone else when they sing, "Great Is Thy Faithfulness, O God My Father."

I told him to read Hebrews. I encouraged him to go to sleep each night reading a good, devotional biography of another sheep. Read Elizabeth Elliot's wonderful biography of Amy Carmichael, the Presbyterian missionary to India (entitled *A Chance to Die*). Read the memoirs and remains of Robert Murray M'Cheyne. Read. Read the letters of Samuel Rutherford put to verse by Faith Cook, which she calls *Grace in Winter*. And read your own life into theirs. For in a real way, they, with the saints of the Bible, are shouting from the sidelines, shouting into the final seconds of a dream about to go bad, shouting what seems "corny" to the rest, but what is real to them: "You got to believe."

> Therefore, since we are surrounded by so great a cloud of witnesses, let us also lay aside every weight, and sin which clings to closely, and let us run with endurance the race that is set before us, looking to Jesus, the founder and perfecter of our faith, who for the joy that was set before him endured the cross, despising the shame, and is seated at the right hand of the throne of God. (Hebrews 12:1–2)

"You got to believe." For God's greatest victories don't always come in regulation. Thank God for overtime.

28

OLD SPICE, HAI KARATÉ, AND THE AROMA OF GOD

Then burn the entire ram on the altar. It
is a burnt offering to the LORD, a pleasing
aroma, an offering made to the LORD by fire.
—Exodus 29:18, NIV

For we are the aroma of Christ to God
among those who are being saved and
among those who are perishing.
—2 Corinthians 2:15

When my father died I was barely six years old. After the funeral, Aunt Eva took me and we went through his possessions. That is a hard thing to do, as some of you know. Well, my dad didn't have many possessions, but of all of the things we found, the one that lasted for almost all of my growing-up years was a bottle of Old Spice cologne. Like many children, I was intrigued by this stuff that my father splashed on his face. When I found it, I took the lid off and took a whiff. It reminded me of my father. So at six years old, I threw some on my face. It tingled and stung a bit on my childish face, but it smelled like my father. I didn't use it for years afterward, but we kept that bottle of cologne in the medicine cabinet. Every time I washed my face I opened the cabinet to check and see if the Old Spice was still there. Aunt Eva never said anything, but she never touched it either. She must have known. The Old Spice was the only thing I had of my father to grow up with.

When I started shaving as an adolescent, Aunt Eva bought me a bottle of "Hai Karaté!" I don't think they make it anymore. It was all right, but it just wasn't the same. It was supposed to make girls go crazy and, according to the ad, one would have to fight them off with playful karate chops. That didn't work either. I can honestly say that I was never attacked by a woman wanting to smell my Hai Karaté. Most importantly, it just didn't have the right smell. It didn't remind me of my father.

The Lord instituted offerings in the Old Testament. We are told that they were sweet-smelling offerings and a pleasing aroma to the Lord. What did that mean? It meant that there was a smell of sacrifice that pleased God. Later we would understand that this was a sign pointing to Jesus Christ. His life and his death were pleasing to God. They were the fulfillment of the Old Testament sacrifices.

But there is a mysterious verse. It says, "We are the aroma of Christ to God among those who are being saved and among those who are perishing" (2 Corinthians 2:15). This tells us that the life of our Lord is now all over us. His blood covers our sins. His life fulfills the perfect law of God on our behalf. Christ has died and risen and ascended. But his life, like my father's Old Spice, is now on us. And his life in us reminds us of our Father. More importantly, it is attractive to those who are being saved. When I am with other believers, when I hear of Christ at work in their lives, I am reminded of my Father.

This happened recently in my ministry. I met with a family and heard a little girl tell how Jesus had come into her heart. We prayed together. And the aroma of Jesus was in that room because of the testimony of that little girl. What a sweet and pleasing aroma of heaven! The verse in Corinthians also says that the aroma of Jesus on his saints is an aroma sensed by those perishing. I guess I could have thought of my father's Old Spice as the aroma of death and associated that smell with death. This is what happens when the gospel goes to those who reject Christ. It is a testimony to their hard-heartedness and smells like death.

The Old Spice became a sign of my father with me growing up. And now, as a believer in the Lord, the savor of Jesus in others' lives helps me. I am in the church because I need to sense his presence. This is where he wants me. And thank God, through the lives of his people, though my Savior is in heaven, he is here with me through the sweet aroma of Christ on all of his people. May you know the aroma of his love this day.

29

OUR KINGDOM OR HIS

s ministers and ministerial students, and as disciples of all kinds, we can get caught up in the kingdom of self, rather than the kingdom of Jesus. We wonder how we can use our gifts, how we can become more fulfilled in our callings, how we could be "used best." This can be good. If we are thinking of the stewardship of time and talents then such questions are relevant. But many times these questions reveal a darker self-absorption.

Recently John Ortberg asked noted spiritual formation leader Dallas Willard about a minister's spiritual life. Here is the conversation quoted from *PreachingNOW.*

> Speaking at last week's National Pastors Convention in San Diego, John Ortberg related a conversation with Dallas Willard in which John posed the question: How do I determine how my spiritual life is doing?

Willard responded by saying you should ask yourself two questions:

Am I growing more or less irritated these days?
Am I growing more or less discouraged these days?

If your answer to those questions is "more," it may be that you have allowed your own ego to become the driving force in your sense of personal and ministry identity. Instead, our lives and ministries should be centered on a vision of God. As Willard observes, "Our life is not an object of deep concern" when we have abandoned ourselves to a vision of the Kingdom of God.[1]

Willard's wisdom touched my heart as something from God. I think of Jesus' words: "For whoever would save his life will lose it, but whoever loses his life for my sake and the gospel's will save it" (Mark 8:35).

That meant something when Jesus called me to be his disciple at the first. I am finding a whole new meaning at this time in my life. Today God seems to be calling me to refocus on his kingdom, not mine.

Maybe this will mean something to you too.

1. Michael Duduit, "From the Editor," *PreachingNOW*, vol. 7, No. 10, March 4, 2008, available online at www.preaching.com/newsletter/preachingnow/11569650/.

30

THE FIELD OF MUSIC

*Cultivating Hearts for
Implanting the Word of God*

*And David assembled all Israel at Jerusalem to
bring up the Ark of the LORD to its place, which
he had prepared for it. —1 Chronicles 15:3*

*Chenaniah, leader of the Levites in music,
should direct the music, for he understood it.
—1 Chronicles 15:22*

I stood and prepared to walk up to the pulpit at the Cedar Falls Bible Conference. I had prepared the text, prayed over it, and asked God to anoint the message. But as I stood there and listened to Diane Susek sing "Jesu, Joy of Man's Desiring," I realized all over again how important the role of music is in preparing hearts to receive God's Word.

In that place where so many of the 1,200 participants were Iowa farmers, I thought about how the fields just outside the campgrounds were metaphors for what her music was doing in our hearts. The lush green fields of tall, healthy corn, standing stalk-to-stalk and row-by-row and growing with visible vitality, would soon be harvested to feed the world.

As Diane sang the beautiful Bach cantata the congregation was stilled by her voice. Her voice, together with the ethereal strains of the organ, caused the powerful words and theology to be sung—rather than spoken—into minds and hearts. Someone said that if your theology doesn't make you sing, it is missing something. Her theology sang that night. And all of us there sang with her in our hearts.

By the time it was my turn to open up Scripture, pray, and preach the unsearchable riches of Christ, the Holy Spirit had done some plowing in that place. The plowing was accomplished through Diane's music. Indeed, I felt that night that rows upon rows of human hearts were opened up by the spade of the Spirit's anointing on the lyrics. Souls were deeply plowed by the implement of a consecrated voice, and minds were cultivated by the holy tools of the organ and piano so that we were prepared to receive the implanted Word of the living God.

This is why David called for Chenaniah, the Levite leader of music, to come when the Ark was being placed in its holy destination. Not only could Chenaniah "do" music, the Bible says "he understood it." The Ark was being brought back to its highest place in the community of Israel. The Ark was a divinely ornate chest that held the tablets of the Ten Commandments, written by the very finger of God, and Aaron's budding rod. Here we see the divine Word of God and the divine activity of God among them. Music needed to reflect those two great themes: the Word of God comes to us by his own hand, and the miraculous promises of God come by his own presence.

Some have put it like this: we sing hymns to God using his very Word, versifying his Word. Isaac Watts' wonderful hymnody, based on a gospel reading of the Psalms, comes to mind for examples of this. The budding rod of Aaron in that Ark reminds us of God's never-failing promises and his wondrous work among his people. So we sing hymns and spiritual songs that encourage us and build us up in the faith based on the faithfulness of God among us, his promises, and the hope we have in the gospel.

We need more musicians who understand that music in worship is deeply connected to the Word and to the presence and power of the gospel. Music gives lyrical and melodic expression to "God with us." It is not entertainment. Music is not "warm up" for the rest of the service nor is it to be used to emotionally manipulate the worshippers. Music in worship is not a replacement for the rest of worship. It is an important part of the liturgical reenactment of the gospel story, week to week, in the service of divine worship. Music really is the accompanying act of worship in which hearts are prepared to receive the implanted Word of God.

King David knew that Chenaniah understood the role of music in worship. Come to think of it, more pastors need to understand it too. For the field of music, rightly cultivated, can produce an unimaginable harvest of good grain in the kingdom of God.

31

SINGING THROUGH
THE SHADOWS

You will make known to me the path of life;
in your presence there is fullness of joy;
at your right hand there are pleasures
forevermore. —Psalm 16:11

Most of the hymns in our hymnal were not produced by professional songwriters or promoted by Nashville producers to get the right sound and sell a commodity. The people who wrote the hymns in our hymnal were writing out of affliction, depression, heartache, spiritual ecstasy from an encounter with God, or a deep movement of the Lord on their souls that produced a joy that could not be contained.

One of my favorite hymn writers is William Cowper (1731–1800). Cowper (pronounced "Cooper") was a contemporary of John Wesley and George Whitefield. He is remembered as one of the greatest poets in the Christian church of any age, but many do not know that he suffered all of his life from a deep, life-controlling depression. Cowper, after being released from an insane asylum, moved to be with a caring family near Olney, England. There he came to be under the ministry of the great evangelical Anglican, John Newton. Cowper, inspired by Newton's doctrine of grace, *Amazing Grace*, turned his troubled heart to heaven and to the wounds of Jesus for sin-sick men like himself and produced some of the most scripturally faithful and poetically inspiring hymns. Cowper sung through the shadows so that he could strain, by holding to Scripture, to see the Light. Worship thus became a defiant act of courage where Cowper stood with Newton and others at the little Olney Parish Church to sing of a grace that would lead them home.

Singing through the shadows is something I think is important for us. Each week as I join the other believers in my church in worshiping the God of grace, I know there are people like Cowper in our midst: pre-teens struggling under the pain of a family coming apart, a brokenhearted young girl whose secret to a best friend has been disclosed, a middle-schooler who didn't make the team, a middle-aged woman hit by news of cancer, a young couple struggling with infertility, a family trying to cope with alcoholism, or a family who must leave their friends and move to find work. Shadows. But in the midst of the shadows, we sing.

I think John Piper summed up the lessons of the hymnists when he wrote about Cowper:

The fruit of William Cowper's affliction is a call to free ourselves from trite and chipper worship. If the Christian life has become the path of ease and fun in the modern West, then corporate worship is the place of increasing entertainment. . . . What William Cowper gives us from his suffering is a vision that sustains the suffering church. Until we suffer we will not be interested. But that day is coming for all of us. And we do well not to wait until it comes before we learn the lessons of Cowper's great hymn, "God Moves in a Mysterious Way":

> Ye fearful saints, fresh courage take,
> The clouds ye so much dread
> Are big with mercy, and shall break
> In blessings on your head.
>
> Blind unbelief is sure to err,
> And scan his work in vain:
> God is his own interpreter,
> And he shall make it plain.[1]

I pray for my own church and for churches everywhere, that those who come into the public worship of Jesus Christ will sing even through the shadows of life, and believe in the Light until he makes it plain. I think the great hymns of the church, including some that are being poured into the souls of men and women in our day, help us to focus on the light of Christ, especially in the shadows. I think worship that employs hymnody grounded in God's Word, composed to God's

1. John Piper, *The Hidden Smile of God: The Fruit of Affliction in the Lives of John Bunyan, William Cowper, and David Brainerd* (Wheaton: Crossway Books, 2001), 167–68.

glory, and arising out of Christian hope, ministers to God's people.

Knowing about the composers, like Cowper, who struggled to sing in the shadows of life, helps us to know that "earnest, joyful worship is the fruit of affliction" and is used of God to bring healing. Worship is an act of giving our best to God. He always beautifies the souls of those who worship him, and in that there is healing. With these things in mind, come to worship again this coming Lord's Day.

32

God, the Restorer

I will restore to you the years that the
swarming locust has eaten, the hopper, the
destroyer, and the cutter, my great army,
which I sent among you. You shall eat
in plenty and be satisfied, and praise the
name of the LORD your God, who has dealt
wondrously with you. —Joel 2:25–26

There is plenty of unhappiness in the world. Plenty of bad news. And much of it, as in the days of Joel, is of our own doing. During that time the Israelites rebelled against God, forgot the Lord, and brought down God's judgment on their land through so many kinds of swarming locusts. But the same God who sent the locusts says he will repay for the years lost. The same God who judged sin graciously satisfied sinners. That means that in God's redemption, there is plenty of happiness being cultivated in this world. That is good news.

This is my story. My life started as a prodigal and ended as a prodigal. During that time, I lost much. But God, so rich in mercy, gave me life—new life—while I was still in trespasses and sins. An old Mike Milton died and a new Mike Milton was born again. While I was still sitting among the ruined fields of locusts, God called me by his grace and ordered me to preach the unsearchable riches of the One who deals wondrously with sinners. And something else: he restored the years the locusts had eaten. In fact, he has done this in so many glorious ways that I will spend eternity thanking him. Let me tell you one way.

When my wife and I wed, we were single parents with my three and her four children. It would be another nine years before John Michael was born and placed in our arms as our son. It would also be another ten years before I would be reunited with children who were removed from my life. I have told that story before (see *What God Starts, God Completes: Help and Hope for Hurting People*[1]), but I have not said just how wondrous is God's restoring grace to my life.

When Mae snapped a photo in 1997 of all three children—all at Gallaudet University in Washington, DC—we were reunited. It was there that a new story began: a story of restoring years that sin and brokenness and heartache had devoured. Those children are now scattered around the country. I could tell you about numerous things: how God kept our hearts together though my children were separated from me, how God

1. Michael A. Milton, *What God Starts, God Completes* (Geanies House, Fearn, Scotland: Christian Focus, 2007).

154

sweetened their hearts toward the Lord though they were not in a Christian home, and how God helped them overcome profound deafness to achieve great academic honor. I could tell you about how God sent Mae to me to be, literally, my voice to these children, and how she invested years of her life returning to college to get a degree in sign language and work with the deaf in Kansas—all in anticipation of reuniting with these children. I could also tell you about how my Aunt Eva, on her deathbed, prayed for this reunion to come about and how it did come within hours of her death, how our hearts have been knitted together, how John Michael has become a beloved brother to them, and how Mae has become a wise, trusted mother for them. I could also tell you how that story is still at work in so many ways. There have been so many blessings and still so much prayer and so much waiting. Let me tell you about Heather.

Heather's own life is a testimony to how God restores what has been lost. Despite all of the challenges that Heather has faced in her family life, her deafness, and her quest for understanding, she has smiled at life even when it has frowned at her. She set her sights on an education at Gallaudet and realized her dream. She dreamed that one day we would be reunited, and we were. She dreamed of a family. She married a godly man, Jimmy. Jimmy is also deaf, but don't tell him this means he has limits! Jimmy graduated from Gallaudet with a degree in biology and now works for the Fish and Game Department of the State of New Jersey. He excels at everything he puts his hand to. And he is a good husband to Heather and an honorable son-in-law. Heather and Jimmy are working hard at building a productive life in New Jersey. They are heroes to me. In all of this, I was reminded again: *he has restored the years the locust has eaten. . . . he has dealt wondrously with you.*

God restores. And he did that ultimately, finally, at the cross of Jesus—the place where locust-eaten fields blossom again.

33

DIAMONDS FOR CHRISTMAS

I am thinking about Advent. I was reading some thoughts by Craig Barnes, Senior Pastor of Shadyside Presbyterian Church in Pittsburgh, Pennsylvania. He talked about how he has been preaching Advent sermons for 25 years and yet he still finds something new in the biblical texts about Jesus' coming. I have been preaching Advent messages for about 15 years. You would think that there are only so many things to say since there are so few passages about the coming of Christ. But truthfully there is more to say about the incarnation of God than could be said by a hundred preachers in a hundred years! Or to be more accurate, thousands upon thousands of preachers in two thousand and nine years (plus or minus five)! I think Dr. Barnes put it best when he wrote, "Preachers are like diamond miners who keep digging at the text until they find a gem they have never before discovered. It is always there waiting for them."

I have been digging around in the first chapter of the gospel of John. I feel like I am a child in the mine with a pickax. I have just hit the mother lode, and I don't know what to do with it! But I do know that we desperately need these diamonds for Christmas. There is so much here about our wonderful Savior! Oh, how can a child bring the diamonds out of the mine and adorn them on the necks of the people in the village? That is the constant dilemma of "diamond mining" preachers! I will continue to labor—praying, searching, testing, and picking away—to bring the right size cut to the saints of my congregation with every coming Lord's Day. We all need nothing more than the simple but glorious truths of the true meaning of Christmas, which are found in the babe who was and is almighty God. With this alone we have more than anything this world has to offer.

I hope you will leave here knowing that you are wearing "diamonds" for Christmas. Let's pray that we will be inspired to do some mining of our own with each coming Advent season!

34

WORSHIPING SOMEONE BIGGER THAN PHIL ... AND OURSELVES

Worthy are you, our Lord and God, to receive
glory and honor and power, for you created
all things, and by your will they existed and
were created.—Revelation 4:11

*W*orship is centered on the worth of another. We must always be focused not on the act of worship, but rather on the eternally divine object of worship.

Several years ago, Carl Reiner and Mel Brooks did a comedy skit called the "2013 Year Old Man." In the skit, Reiner interviewed Brooks, who played the old gentleman. At one point Reiner asked the old man, "Did you always believe in the Lord?"

Brooks replied, "No. We had a guy in our village named Phil, and for a time we worshiped him."

Reiner: "You worshiped a guy named Phil? Why?"

Brooks: "Because he was big and mean, and he could break you in two with his bare hands!"

Reiner: "Did you have prayers?"

Brooks: "Yes, would you like to hear one? 'O Phil, please don't be mean and hurt us or break us in two with your bare hands.'"

Reiner: "So when did you start worshiping the Lord?"

Brooks: "Well, one day a big thunderstorm came up, and a lightning bolt hit Phil. We gathered around and saw that he was dead. Then we said to one another, 'There's somethin' bigger than Phil!'"

Correction to Mel Brooks: "There's not just 'somethin',' but *someone* bigger than Phil . . . and ourselves."

Delighting in the glory of the one who made us and redeemed us through the blood of his Son, Jesus Christ, is what our worship is all about.

William Temple, an Anglican bishop of another generation, wrote, "Worship is the submission of all our nature to God. It is the quickening of conscience by his holiness, the nourishment of the mind with his truth, the purifying of the imagination of his beauty, the opening of the heart to his love, the surrender of the will to his purpose."

Each and every week, we have this opportunity to surrender our will to his in a public way. We follow the well-worn path of joining with each other in the old familiar "family language" of common worship: the language of Scripture, hymns, creeds, and prayers. This family language is expressed best as a common language that gives united voice to our worship of the one who is greater than ourselves. There has been much written in our time about generational worship, seeker-friendly worship, and so forth. The movement has brought us many helpful insights and provoked healthy reflection of being authentic in our service to the Lord. But sometimes, little is presented about sacrificing our lives and our preferences in order to come together as one people united. The Bible says nothing about style, but it says a lot about the motivation of our hearts and about the one we worship. All sides need to remember this.

God-centered, God-glorifying worship and worship that is in spirit and in truth is what I call "living worship." Such language avoids the trendy descriptions that have appeared in the last decades and doesn't address expressions or styles. Descriptions of styles take us away from the substance of worship and from the one we worship. Style language centers only on expressions of worship. Too often churches get all hung up on expressions of worship (which vary) rather than principles and elements of worship, which are set by God in his Word. And there is nothing that unites us more or better than what Michael W. Smith sang about: "Ancient Words." Together—and that is the important word for public worship—*together* we come, from different generations, varying backgrounds, a myriad of experiences, and a multitude of ideas.

We must never lose the commonality of worship or our unity at the expense of personal preferences. Our unity comes from the one we worship. So again, we come with "ancient words" to worship the one who is greater, the one who is the focus of our worship, our lives, our community, and our very minds and hearts. For nothing else and no one else is worthy.

Let us thus submit our lives again today to the one who is greater than ourselves. Let us worship our Lord Jesus Christ in spirit and in truth according to his Word.

35

GETTING UNDER YOUR SKIN

And being found in human form, he
humbled himself by becoming obedient to
the point of death, even death on a cross.
—Philippians 2:8

C an we talk about the incarnation other than just during Christmas? We should. The incarnation, when God took upon himself human flesh, is a deep but practical doctrine that has significant everyday implications. (All doctrine is "practical"—it is all "faith for living," if you will.)

I will describe just one application of how the incarnation is practical, because it comes up in my counseling ministry almost every single week: incarnation and marriage.

The key to a great marriage is imitating Christ in our relationships with each other. This is the force of Ephesians 5:1: "Therefore be imitators of God, as beloved children." Then Paul works that out in marriage when he comes to verse 21: ". . . submitting to one another out of reverence for Christ."

This mutual submission, we learn, is based upon the model of Christ and the church. As a believer surrenders to Christ, so a wife surrenders to her husband. As Jesus gave himself up for the Church, so a husband is to give himself up for his wife. The key to this is *incarnation*. A simple way to think of incarnation is simply "living in another person's skin."

Jesus, the eternal God, did this in human form, Paul tells us in Philippians. We do this in marriage as we seek to live in our spouse's skin. For instance, in Christian marriage, we can no longer say, "Well, this is the way I am, and you are going to have to learn to just like it or leave it!" Wrong. If God had taken that kind of approach in dealing with us, we would be eternally hopeless!

We are to imitate God who came to us in the incarnation. Therefore, we say, "God made me like this, but love compels me to leave that kind of attitude and take upon myself your attitude, your way of thinking, your predispositions." We cannot say, "This is my Myers-Briggs personality type, baby; get used to it!" We say, "What is *your* Meyers-Briggs personality type? I want to move out of my comfort zone and seek to identify with you in yours." Imagine what might happen when both parties are seeking incarnational living in their marriage. Of course, this applies to all of our relationships. Imagine that kind of approach in friendships or in relationships at church.

We read in Proverbs 15:33: "The fear of the LORD is instruction in wisdom, and humility comes before honor."

Christ's humility is supremely displayed in his incarnation. It brought about great honor as the resurrected Christ ascended to be the reigning Christ. Humility in our relationships brings about such honor. Incarnational relationships produce happy, joyful, and fruitful relationships in marriage, yes, but also in all other relationships of our lives.

"Be imitators of God." Become a servant to another today, as Christ became a servant to reach you. You will be amazed at how getting under another person's skin, to put it in a biblical way, will help others get under yours.

Beloved, let us love one another.

36

RICHARD BAXTER ON COUNSELING: CASES OF CONSCIENCE

Pray also for me, that whenever I open my mouth, words may be given me so that I will fearlessly make known the mystery of the gospel, for which I am an ambassador in chains. Pray that I may declare it fearlessly, as I should. —Ephesians 6:19–20, NIV

The English Puritans referred to counseling as dealing with "cases of conscience." The pastor who helps us most in understanding this great work of the gospel is Richard Baxter. Sometimes before I preach, I pray, "Let me preach as if never to preach again and as a dying man to dying men." That is a direct quote from this great English Puritan from the 17th century. He was a dedicated servant of the Lord and an accomplished pastor to pastors. Through his classic work, *The Reformed Pastor*, Baxter provides great assistance as he deals with the cases of conscience. He advises:

> We must be ready to give advice to inquirers, who come to us with cases of conscience; especially the great case which the Jews put to Peter, and the gaoler to Paul and Silas, "What must we do to be saved?"[1]

And he writes:

> A minister is not to be merely a public preacher, but to be known as a counselor for their souls, as the physician is for their bodies, and the lawyer for their estates: so that each man who is in doubts and straits, may bring his case to him for resolution; as Nicodemus came to Christ, and as it was usual with the people of old to go to the priest, "whose lips must keep knowledge, and at whose mouth they must ask the law, because he is the messenger of the Lord of hosts."[2]

This is a great reminder to you and me. There are many things that come to me in a week, but the two things I do each and every week of my life, except for retreats and vacations, are counsel and preach.

Pastoral counseling is one of the greatest sources of fulfillment and at the same time one of the greatest sources of burden. It literally drives me to my knees.

1. Richard Baxter, *The Reformed Pastor* (1655, repr.; London: The Religious Tract Society, 2006), 81.
2. Ibid., 81–83.

Good! Some have taught that the pastor must assume some sort of vocational—or clinical, if you will—posture in dealing with so many cases, or he will be weighed down with sorrow. I understand that caution, and there is truth in it. For if the "wounded healer" is not healed enough to reach for the divine remedy, then he is of no help to the afflicted. Although it is difficult not to carry those cases of conscience with me, I am not sure I want it any other way. And I suspect you prefer a pastor to ponder things in his heart, too. Baxter says that he cannot imagine preaching without visiting and being out and about with the people and their needs, or hearing of their struggles in his office. Again, I feel the same way. People's lives, their struggles, the pain and passion and joys and sorrows of life, should shape my heart and the heart of every preacher, so that when we climb into our pulpits on Sunday morning, our messages and worship leadership reflect both God's Word and man's condition.

Pastors need your prayer support for this ministry. Paul asked for this in his ministry several times. The request in Ephesians 6 is particularly poignant because he asked for prayer following a teaching on the reality of spiritual darkness and of our need to put on the full armor of God. All pastors need this. I feel the need of prayer and wisdom as I seek to fulfill my ministry in the cases of conscience that come before me.

That leads me to a main point that I want to make in this little epistle: Come to us! I speak for pastors everywhere when I say we are here not only for public ministry, but also for private ministry. In our church we are blessed with capable assistants who share in this divinely ordained burden and joy, and I trust that your church has such assistants in place too. I receive Baxter's advice and invite the congregation to come. He wrote,

> But as the people have become unacquainted with this office of the ministry, and with their own duty and necessity in this respect, it belongs to us to acquaint them with it, and publicly to press them to come to us for advice about the great concerns of their souls. We must not only be willing to take the trouble, but should draw it upon ourselves, by inviting them to come.[3]

That is what I want to do in my congregation, and what I hope pastors everywhere are working toward. Sometimes hearing these "cases of conscience" happens in our offices. Sometimes it happens in a bleacher at a ball game. Sometimes it happens at the front door of the church, as I greet people on Sunday. You must know that this is a vital part of ministry that pastors, no matter how much joy it brings them, need your prayers to fulfill.

3. Ibid., 83–85.

37

MORE TALES FROM A LOCUST SURVIVOR

"I will restore to you the years that the swarming locust has eaten." —Joel 2:25

When I was a child I used to gather locust shells and take them to Aunt Eva as a present.

Recently I introduced a sermon with a story about presenting locust shells to Aunt Eva. The locust shell, in the story, represented a testimony. The empty shell was once filled with a locust, representing the presence of something hurtful in life. And the act of offering that empty shell represented worship to God with the very marks of his testimony in my life.

I know it is a bit "icky"! But grace can be messy. And the process of being birthed into the kingdom of Christ, into the hands of a loving Savior, is sometimes messy too. By the way, how would you feel if someone watched as you emerged from sin and shame into a new life of freedom? Even as I write I feel a bit guilty for showing this most personal moment in the locust's life!

Well, my friend, God is good. He will restore to you the years the locust has eaten. I pray that through his Word, and by his Spirit's powerful working, you know that you are "emerging" like the poor little locust from the old shell or the pain of sin. This can only happen when the resurrection power of Jesus supernaturally takes hold in your life. This is also the power that will raise you from the dead. Imagine that photo!

38

THE CHURCH MILITANT AND
THE CHURCH TRIUMPHANT

In all of our thoughts, all of our actions,
in every part of our character, the ruling
principle that motivates and guides us
should be the desire to follow Christ in doing
the will of the Father. This is the high road
we must follow in the pursuit of holiness.
—Jerry Bridges

One of the greatest books I have ever read is *Holiness* by J. C. Ryle (1816–1900), the old Bishop of Liverpool. A memorable part of the book is that, after showing us how grace brings us positional holiness, it demonstrates how grace brings us practical holiness. This too is a mark of authentic Christianity. Receiving what God has done for us in Christ, the believer is empowered to "walk." The church is called the "Church Militant." E. Cobham Brewer (1810–1897) in his *Dictionary of Phrase and Fable* (1898) defined the phrase in this way: "The Church on earth means the whole body of believers, who are said to be 'waging the war of faith against the world, the flesh, and the devil.' It is therefore militant, or in warfare."

We can agree with Charles Wesley who spoke of how we "wrestle and fight and pray." We do that through exercising the ordinary means of grace: Word, sacrament, and prayer. We encourage ourselves in the Word of God by studying and memorizing God's Word, by immersing our minds in the things of God, by meditating on the glory of Christ, by attending worship, Sunday school, Bible studies, and small group meetings, and by having personal times with Christ. As we come to the Sacraments, to taste the bread and drink from the cup, we are fed and strengthened in Christ. As the covenantal waters of baptism fall upon the heads of others in sacred assembly, our hearts are warmed by the reality that Christ's love has come to us. We remember that his anointing and sealing are upon our lives. Through prayer, in public and private, we bring our struggles to the Lord. And through all of these things we carry on as the Church Militant.

One day, when we pass from this life, we shall become the Church Triumphant. The Church Triumphant is, and I quote Brewer again, "Those who are dead and gone to their rest, having fought the fight and triumphed, they belong to the Church triumphant in heaven." We shall join that triumphant band of victorious believers, but not quite yet.

While we have breath in us it is our calling to keep in step with the Spirit. It is our calling, having been grounded in grace, to apply and live out that grace. With every struggle, there is a call for our Captain. With every encounter with the reality of our sinfulness, there is the need to go again to the Redeemer. With every failure there is not retreat, but a return to the front line. This is why we gather together. This is why we are told not to forsake the assembling of ourselves. This is why we sing to encourage each other in song. This is why we sing Charles Wesley's "Soldiers of Christ, Arise."

> To keep your armor bright, attend with constant
> care,
> Still walking in your Captain's sight, and watch-
> ing unto prayer.
> Ready for all alarms, steadfastly set your face,
> And always exercise your arms, and use your
> every grace.

175

39

MICHAEL MEDVED, MOBILIZATION, FIRST PRESBYTERIAN CHURCH, AND THE GREAT BALANCING ACT

Some Thoughts as I Pray

*As for you, always be sober-minded, endure
suffering, do the work of an evangelist, fulfill
your ministry. —2 Timothy 4:5*

I got to thinking about the military during a trip
to Jackson, Mississippi, where I went to preach
in chapel and to counsel seminary students, on
behalf of the U.S. Army Chaplaincy. That was how I

spent my two-day commitment to the Army Reserves during the month of the trip. Not a big deal when you think of what others were doing and continue to do on behalf of the army. Being on the trip made me realize that we need more pastors to minister to troops in a reserve capacity. Why would I encourage men to set out on a course of balancing family and civilian ministry with the increasing demands of the United States armed services? Although it is a balancing act and my wife and son have sacrificed much for me to be able to do it, I think I can make the case to these fledgling pastors that it is worth it.

First of all, it was not coincidental that one of the church elders gave me a CD just a couple of days prior to this chaplain recruiting trip. I was emboldened by this recording, which was a recent speech given by the noted film critic, Michael Medved. Speaking before the student body at Hillsdale College, Mr. Medved helped clarify our current national and even international situation.

Essentially, Mr. Medved reminded us that we have gone through what he sees as World War III (the Cold War), and now we are in World War IV (the struggle for civilization against radical Islamic fascism). You can argue with him, but it made a lot of sense to me. Speaking about our own current conflict, one of the points he made was that while our society is being somewhat disrupted as men and women are called to serve our nation in armed resistance to this war, on many fronts we have done this before.

Being a film critic he was interested in how this plays out in Hollywood. In the "good old days" of Hollywood, before the Hollywood elite became as anti-American as they seem to be today, actors like Jimmy Stewart, Clark Gabel, and Henry Fonda voluntarily disrupted their stellar (and lucrative) careers to fight in Europe or the Pacific. This was more than just self-promotion. Jimmy Stewart, for instance, flew more than 50 dangerous missions over Nazi German occupied territory. Medved also pointed out that there were men in other forms of entertainment who served, like Ted Williams, arguably the greatest hitter in baseball history, who left the Big Leagues after just batting .406 to fight in World War II. Ted Williams once again fought for his country during the Korean Conflict. What Michael Medved was saying was this: when our nation is threatened, there have always been those who were willing to step up and fight, even when it meant leaving promising careers to do so. We are in a war today. There are others stepping up. And we need them as much today as we did in 1942.

The balancing act of pastor and chaplain is worth it, and it is not without gospel precedent. Many others have done it. Richard Baxter, the great Puritan pastor, was a chaplain to Parliamentary forces during the English Civil War. He served his country while he pastored the large parish church of Kidderminster, England. The founder of Covenant College and Covenant Seminary, Dr. Robert Rayburn, was a parish pastor-turned-airborne-chaplain, who parachuted into Nazi territory with his unexpected flock during World War II. There are stories to tell of pastor-chaplains in the Revolutionary War, the Civil War, and every other conflict we have experienced. And many are living this balancing act today. I am thinking of the Rev. Randy Nabors, the esteemed New City Fellowship PCA pastor, who has done this through a 30-year career. I am thinking as well of men in my own congregation, as well as congregations across the country, who have done it, and are doing it right now. To minister the gospel of Christ to a congregation of civilians is one of the highest honors in my life. To do so, as I also minister the gospel to men and women in uniform, is a double blessing.

The balancing act—vocational life and evangelism— is a way of life for all of us who follow the Nazarene. We are people of one holy passion that works out in at least a couple of vocations: the vocation we have to support our families, to contribute to the common good, and to produce things that we need in order to establish a society. This is the will of God. As his people we are also called to do the work of an evangelist. For a minister it means using every gift, every opportunity, and every hour available to advance the kingdom of our Lord Jesus Christ in the lives of men and women. That is what I desire to do with my whole life and every gift and opportunity given me: to offer the free gospel of God's grace in Jesus Christ so that an innumerable host will be safe in the arms of Jesus on the day when he returns. And for those who will never wear a pastor's robe or a chaplain's cross, it means doing the same thing, in different ways, unique to their own callings and gifts.

I went into this civilian-military balancing act in order to reach out to young, wayfaring men in uniform, who are seeking to find their way through life. I know all about those boys because I was one of them. It is a way for me to give back to the country that has given me so much. It is a way for me to honor my own father who gave his whole life as an officer on the sea to protect this nation. And it is a way—a much smaller way than army infantrymen or naval line officers or marines—to fight the foes that threaten freedom. Others are called as farmers, plumbers, attorneys, doctors, business people, and teachers, to reach beyond—nay, through—that calling to find ways to proclaim that the kingdom of God is at hand. Each of us is called to do the work of an evangelist, to share Christ in this world through our lives while there is breath in our bodies. Jesus must be the all-consuming priority of our lives. Sharing his life and his teaching with others is our vocation.

This is what I was thinking about as I preached the Word of God first in a Methodist and then in a Presbyterian seminary in Jackson. I relayed to those studying God's Word that it is a tough balancing act. But it is worth it in order to do the work of an evangelist.

It is what I was thinking afterward, as I went home, kissed my wife, and spent time with my son. And it is what I continue to think about as I prepare each week to preach the unsearchable riches of Jesus Christ to the precious flock of Jesus at Chattanooga.

This is the life. It is often a balancing act, but it is always worth it.

40

COSMOLOGY, THEOLOGY, AND THE ARROGANCE OF THE MODERN

Cosmology is "the area of science that aims at a comprehensive theory of the structure and evolution of the entire physical universe—the cosmos, which is the totality of energy and matter." Theology is the study of God. One is popular today. One is not. One subject is interesting. One is derided as stuffy, divisive, or even irrelevant. Even many in the church seem to approach these two great matters in this way.

Actually, we learn from the Bible that cosmology *is* theology. For God created the heavens and the earth. You cannot really speak of the cosmos without speaking of God. There is a place in the Word of God that brings the two together. I speak of Isaiah 66:1–6. It is the end of the great evangelistic book of the Old Testament. And Isaiah concludes this book as he started it, with a vision of God speaking to Israel. In that last chapter, one final blow is delivered to a sinning people. It begins, "Heaven is my throne, and the earth is my footstool." There it is. Cosmology and theology. Cosmology: the universe. Theology: God.

The universe was conceived of in many ways by ancient peoples. But Israel could conceive of it only through God's revelation. Moses told them that God had created the heavens and the earth. One of my favorite verses in the entire Bible is Genesis 1:16: "he made the stars also" (KJV). No big deal. He *simply* flung "billions and billions" (as the atheist Carl Sagan used to say) of burning spheres into space. I love it. This God is the one who says, "Heaven is my throne."

In the metaphor of Isaiah 66 (filled with divine sarcasm, much like Psalm 50), God reclines on the universe and kicks his feet up on the earth. God says this because he wants Israel to know who he is and who they are. He says that a temple cannot hold him (66:1b) and blood sacrifices of animals cannot appease him or bring him pleasure (66:3–4). He wants them to bow before him in faith and to respond to him in love as their Creator. He tells them, then, that the one "to whom [he] will look" is the one who is "humble and contrite in spirit and trembles at my word" (66:2b).

At this time Israel is not humble or contrite, and the people have ignored the Word of God. God is not only insulted by such pride, but man is injured by it. The lesson in cosmology and theology is undeniable: get back to the Word. Fear—let us not diminish the meaning of that word—*fear* God. When that happens, things will change. The nation will return to the Lord.

People get right with God when they see God for who he is (the mighty God) and see themselves and their little religious acts as what they are (nothing except offensive to God). Then, add to that a love that condescends in the midst of that sin and offers himself up to those sinners, through Jesus Christ on the cross, and you have a picture of a great God and a loving God coming to sinful people. And when those things get lined up, you have revival. Then you have blessings. But it all begins with fearing God's Word.

How is your cosmology? How is your theology? How are these things in our nation today? I thought about these questions as I read more about the latest rage sweeping the nation: same-sex marriage. This is the height of arrogance, of ignoring the plain teaching of the Bible. Without repentance there will come divine judgment. This is abhorrent to God, but so are the abortions in our nation, and the vulgar, godless, Christ-defying ideas and images that are pumped into the sacred hearths and homes of our country, like raw sewage being pumped into the Sistine Chapel. When you do away with your "creed," your "code" quickly crumbles. When God's Word is ignored, the breakdown of a society is not surprising; it is inevitable. That is what we are seeing in our nation. Is that not what we see in the church, also?

Remember, God is speaking not to the heathen but to Israel. When we do not tremble before the Word of God, we end up "doing what [is] evil in [God's] eyes" (66:4b). I must repent. We must cry out and tremble before him. For the sensate culture of this present age is often found in our thoughts and suppositions. My beloved in the Lord, we need revival in our time. And it must begin with a people humbled before the Word of God, a people who tremble at his Word. God said of Israel: "When I called, no one answered, when I spoke they did not listen" (66:4a). Oh, may we hear. May we answer. And may our answer be, "Yes, Lord, we shall come before you as unto the God who created us; the God who loved us in our sin and sent Jesus Christ to be punished for our arrogance and pride. Yes, Lord, we are listening. Yes, Lord, we fear your Word. We honor your Word. We prize your Word. And Jesus, O God, Jesus your Son is our only hope. Forgive us and send the Spirit of Jesus into our hearts, our hearth, and our nation. Forgive us and renew our minds through your Word."

Charles Haddon Spurgeon said that all of the Scriptures "make a beeline to the Cross." And in his Word, cosmology and theology converge at the cross, where God came down and died for our defiance. Do these two great ideas not also converge in the brokenhearted sinner who cries out to God and receives Jesus Christ as Lord? I still believe that the light shines best in the darkness and that God has not forgotten us. Let us not forget him. Let us tremble before his Word.

41

OF PASSION PLAYS
AND THE WORD OF GOD

I began to think about the role of images in our culture while planning to see Mel Gibson's much-anticipated film *The Passion of Christ*. Like many of you, I had heard wonderful things about it. But I had also heard enough that, while my son was being taught about the suffering of Christ for his sins, I was concerned that the graphic portrayal of the crucifixion may be too much for a nine-year-old. The Word of God, though, is clear, and all of us should remember the graphic words that are given to us in the Old Testament.

> But I am a worm and not a man,
>> scorned by mankind and despised by the
>> people.
> All who see me mock me;
>> they make mouths at me; they hang their
>> heads;
> He trusts in the LORD; let him deliver him;
>> let him rescue him, for he delights in him!

Yet you are he who took me from the womb;
>you made me trust you at my mother's
>breasts.
On you was I cast from my birth,
>and from my mother's womb you have been
>my God.
Be not far from me,
>for trouble is near,
>and there is none to help. (Psalm 22:6–11)

And in Isaiah 53:

But he was wounded for our transgressions;
>he was crushed for our iniquities;
upon him was the chastisement that brought us
>peace,
>and with his stripes we are healed. (v. 5)

There are some things about this and other portrayals of Christ and the Bible that I want to address. My thoughts are caution, with no attempt to bind conscience or throw cold water on what many see as a cultural opportunity for the gospel. I have no qualms with the film, but the warnings of Scripture about certain things convict the conscience of this pastor to raise these matters to the beloved sheep of our Lord. One has to do with type and image, and the other has to do with means and ends.

In the days before the Word of God brought reformation and revival to the English-speaking world and in Europe, the people were cut off from the Bible. The language of the priests was not their language and though many believed, they were denied the expository preaching that many of us today take for granted. The poor folk had to rely upon traveling passion plays to receive the Word of God. The passion plays brought images that (frequently but not always) reflected the drama of the Bible, but no teaching. (This is not to say there can be no teaching in drama, but there is no *kerygma* or proclamation of the Word in it.)

It was John Wycliffe who recognized that there could be no revival in mere plays. There had to be not just an image, but also the taught Word of God. In order for the Word of God to go forth, the Bible had to be translated into the tongue, the "heart language," of the people. So Wycliffe set about his famous and glorious work. Revival followed. The same thing happened with Luther and Calvin and in the American revivals. Revival did not come with image, but with the Word of God taught.

This brings us to consider one of the reasons that God called for his people to do something that no one else was doing—to worship him in our minds, not with our eyes. The Second Commandment—make no images—has at its core an idea that calls us to refrain from imaging God and to think about him only as he reveals himself to us. The late Neil Postman, in his *Amusing Ourselves to Death*, warned about this. He wrote, "The God of the Jews was to exist in the Word and through the Word, an unprecedented conception requiring the highest order of abstract thinking. Iconography thus became blasphemy so that a new kind of God could enter a culture. People like ourselves who are in the process of converting their culture from word-centered to image-centered might profit by reflecting on this Mosaic injunction."[1]

Of course, in Jesus, we have God revealed in *form*, in *image*, if you will. And the debate goes on

1. Neil Postman, *Amusing Ourselves to Death: Public Discourse in the Age of Show Business* (New York: Viking, 1985), 9.

with believers over what constitutes image making of any of the persons of the Godhead since Jesus has come. But one thing is for sure: God has called us to be people of the Word. And this leads me to this final thought concerning the movie.

Movies such as Mel Gibson's *The Passion of Christ* must not be asked to do things *by themselves* that God does not intend. Image alone did not bring revival in medieval Christianity. (Postman's work on communications suggests that we are in a cultural regression— back to pre-Reformation days, when type and reading and abstract thinking were non-existent.) Image alone cannot be counted on to convey deep spiritual truth about the atonement of Christ. We are called to go and "teach them whatsoever I have commanded." Surely, movies and other images may aid us in this. But eventually a person must be taught who Jesus really is, why he came, and how his grace draws us to worship him and to learn more of him in his Word. John Piper has produced a book, *The Passion of Christ: 50 Reasons Why He Came to Die.* This will be helpful, I am sure.

As people's attention is arrested by the drama, I pray they will be drawn to the Bible. For there the Word of God tells us about how even Christ in his resurrected body, the very image of God, modeled how truth is to be communicated. "Did not our hearts burn within us while he talked to us on the road, while he opened to us the Scriptures?" (Luke 24:32).

As millions see the film, may millions recognize him and then may his disciples, in his name, be bold to open the Scriptures to this lost generation. For he is known only through the work of his Spirit.

190

42

FAMILY DEVOTIONS AND THE COTTARS' SATURDAY NIGHT

I wrote the following letter to my family after our nightly devotions, which focused on 1 John. Our questions about one verse prompted us to continue our studies. I want to open the door to our home and our lives for just a bit and draw your attention to family devotions.

My dear wife and son,

I did some research this morning on the passage that we read last night.

> I write these things to you who believe in the name of the Son of God that you may know that you have eternal life. And this is the confidence that we have toward him, that if we ask anything according to his will he hears us. And if we know that he hears

us in whatever we ask, we know that we have the requests that we have asked of him. If anyone sees his brother committing a sin not leading to death, he shall ask, and God will give him life—to those who commit sins that do not lead to death. There is sin that leads to death; I do not say that one should pray for that. All wrongdoing is sin, but there is sin that does not lead to death. (1 John 5:13–17)

Admittedly that verse about the "sin that leads unto death" needs special attention. We talked about it last night, and I think we were led by the Spirit to understand it well. I thought about it some more in personal devotions this morning (wonderful how our family devotions and my own devotions have so often merged). Here is what John Calvin wrote about this:

We ought not rashly to conclude that any one has brought on himself the judgment of eternal death; on the contrary, love should dispose us to hope well. But if the impiety of some appear to us not other-wise than hopeless, as though the Lord pointed it out by the finger, we ought not to contend with the just judgment of God, or seek to be more merciful than he is. (John Calvin, "Commentary on the First Epistle of John, 5:13," Accordance Bible Software, 2008).

And Matthew Henry (you know how I love that old Puritan Presbyterian) wrote:

We should pray for others, as well as for ourselves, beseeching the Lord to pardon and recover the fallen, as well as to relieve the tempted and afflicted. And let us be truly thankful that no sin, of which any

one truly repents, is unto death. (Matthew Henry,
Commentary [Condensed], Accordance, 2008)

So we see that while there are such sins that lead to
death, we are to pray for others no matter their condition until at last death itself becomes God's judgment.
Then, seeing his judgment, we have no other prayers
than to commend one to the justice and wisdom of
God.

I wanted to clear this up for us so that we leave the
passage (and the book of 1 John) in good shape, so to
speak. It is a hard passage but an important passage,
for its truth teaches us:

1. Our understanding of the seriousness of sin and
   how we ought to run frequently to our Lord for
   mercy and cleansing of our daily failings before
   him, and plead the blood of Jesus;
2. The severe judgment of God and how this ought
   to work a godly fear in our hearts lest we fall
   into discipline or even judgment under the living God;
3. The right objects of our prayers—how we should
   and should not pray;
4. The mercy of God that reaches to the worst
   sinner and how we should never give up on the
   most vile offender.

I write to you because I think that our devotions are as
important as a Sunday school class or preparing for a
sermon. I am dealing with your souls so intertwined
with my own, the "flesh of my flesh and bone of my
bone."

193

I often think of our devotional times as the power that Burns of Scotland wrote about in "The Cottar's Saturday Night." There in that simple cottage, in the darkness of that valley in the towering Highlands, a simple light in the cottage revealed a power that not only forged but held together the greatest empire on earth.

Here are lines that I have cherished and want to share with you, those who have tasted of the beauties of our family devotions these many years:

> The chearfu' Supper done, wi' serious face,
> They, round the ingle, form a circle wide;
> The Sire turns o'er, wi' patriarchal grace,
> The big ha'-Bible, ance his Father's pride:
> His bonnet rev'rently is laid aside,
> His lyart haffets wearing thin and bare;
> Those strains that once did sweet in Zion glide,
> He wales a portion with judicious care;
> "And let us worship God!" he says with solemn
>   air.
> They chant their artless notes in simple guise,
> They tune their hearts, by far the noblest aim:
> Perhaps Dundee's wild-warbling measures rise,
> Or plaintive Martyrs, worthy of the name;
> Or noble Elgin beets the heaven-ward flame,
> The sweetest far of Scotia's holy lays:
> Compar'd with these, Italian trills are tame;
> The tickl'd ears no heart-felt raptures raise;
> Nae unison hae they, with our Creator's praise.
> The priest-like Father reads the sacred page,
> Then kneeling down to heaven's eternal King,
> The Saint, the Father, and the Husband prays:
> Hope "springs exulting on triumphant wing,"

That thus they all shall meet in future days:
There, ever bask in uncreated rays,
No more to sigh, or shed the bitter tear,
Together hymning their Creator's praise,
In such society, yet still more dear;
While circling Time moves round in an eternal
    sphere.
From scenes like these, old Scotia's grandeur
    springs,
That makes her lov'd at home, rever'd abroad.[1]

Oh may our light never go out in our cottage!

I love you both,
Your happy husband and blessed father

---

1. http://www.electricscotland.com/burns/cotters.html.

43

STORMS BLOW IN SO OUR PRAYERS MAY GO UP

As of this writing, Hurricane Gustav is just beginning to hurl itself against the already battered and worn Gulf Coast, threatening the rebuilding efforts that have gone on for three years since Hurricane Katrina. So we all pause to pray. We pray for God's protection for the courageous first responders who remained after 1.9 million people were heroically evacuated. We pray for the 10,000 plus souls who remained in New Orleans, plus those scattered along the Mississippi coast. We pray for those dislodged from their homes. We pray for our nation.

Storms, real ones, metaphoric ones, personal ones, national ones, drive us to prayer and to God like nothing else. We remember that storms were common to the disciples of Jesus.

> And behold, there arose a great storm on the sea,
> so that the boat was being swamped by the waves;
> but he was asleep. (Matthew 8:24)

> And they went and woke him, saying, "Master, Mas-
> ter, we are perishing!" And he awoke and rebuked
> the wind and the raging waves, and they ceased,
> and there was a calm. (Luke 8:24)

St. Paul, while being taken by government officials to Rome, encountered a storm.

> And when the ship was caught and could not face
> the wind, we gave way to it and were driven along.
> (Acts 27:15)

An angel visited Paul, and he was divinely warned that the ship must run aground.

> Paul said to the centurion and the soldiers, "Unless
> these men stay in the ship, you cannot be saved."
> (Acts 27:31)

Salvation for the frightened sailor-disciples slept in the ship beside them. God was there. His power is available even when he sleeps. He is there. For us the best place to be is beside him in prayer. We must remember, as Paul instructed the sailors of his vessel, "Unless these men stay in the ship, you cannot be saved."

This is a time for ministers of the gospel to turn the hearts of their people to God. It is a time for us to be in the ship. We look beyond the Federal Emergency Management Agency (FEMA) and the National Guard. These are gifts from God for the common good, and we thank God for them and for those who labor for the good of mankind. Yet we seek Jesus in this storm. And we say to the nation, "There is no salvation outside of the ship where Christ is."

I have been reading about the orders of worship that were written for *The Book of Common Prayer*. I found one order of worship that seems so appropriate for days like today. I can only imagine a wise old sea captain, who has seen such storms and has known the power of God in the storm, calling "all hands on deck." He orders the men to remove their hats and bow their heads, and he calls on the chaplain to pray. I offer this, taken from The Armed Forces Hymnal (Washington, D.C.: Armed Forces Chaplain's Board, 1940) for all of us who are moved to pray for the storm that looms and the storms that might come.

THOU O Lord, who stillest the raging of the sea, hear;

hear us, and save us, that we perish not.
O blessed Saviour, who didst save thy disciples ready to perish in a storm, hear us, and save us, we beseech thee. Lord, have mercy upon us.

Christ, have mercy upon us.
Lord, have mercy upon us.
O Lord, hear us.

O Christ, hear us. God the Father, God the Son, God the Holy Ghost, have mercy upon us, save us now and evermore. Amen. Our Father, who art in heaven, Hallowed be thy Name. Thy kingdom come. Thy will be done on earth, As it is in heaven. Give us this day our daily bread. And forgive us our trespasses, As we forgive those who trespass against us. And lead us not into temptation; But deliver us from evil. Amen. When there shall be imminent danger, as many as can be

199

spared from necessary service in the ship shall be called together, and make an humble confession of their sin to God: In which, every one ought seriously to reflect upon those particular sins of which his conscience shalt accuse him; saying as followeth, ALMIGHTY God, Father of our Lord Jesus Christ, Maker of all things, Judge of all men; We acknowledge and bewail our manifold sins and wickedness, Which we from time to time most grievously have committed, By thought, word, and deed, against thy Divine Majesty, provoking most justly thy wrath and indignation against us. We do earnestly repent, and are heartily sorry for these our misdoings; the remembrance of them is grievous unto us; the burden of them is intolerable. Have mercy upon us, Have mercy upon us, most merciful Father; for thy Son our Lord Jesus Christ's sake, forgive us all that is past; and grant that we may ever hereafter serve and please thee in newness of life, to the honour and glory of thy Name; Through Jesus Christ our Lord. Amen.

ALMIGHTY God, our heavenly Father, who of his great mercy hath promised forgiveness of sins to all those who with hearty repentance and true faith turn unto him; Have mercy upon you; pardon and deliver you from all your sins; confirm and strengthen you in all goodness, and bring you to everlasting life; through Jesus Christ our Lord. Amen.

> Whate'er my God ordains is right:
> he is my Friend and Father;
> he suffers naught to do me harm,
> Though many storms may gather,
> Now I may know both joy and woe,
> Some day I shall see clearly
> That he hath loved me dearly.
> AMEN.

44

A THEOLOGY OF
THE HONEYMOONERS

Come to me, all who labor and are heavy laden, and I will give you rest. —Matthew 11:28

Jackie Gleason was not a Christian as far as I know. In fact, his reputation for sin may or may not have been as big as that of Reginald Van Gleason, III, one of his famous over-the-top characters. Mr. Gleason was probably a mixture of good and bad, which means that, like all of us, he needed a righteousness not his own. I do not know if he found that in Jesus Christ. I leave that to a just and most merciful God. May the Lord have mercy on his soul.

But recently, my family and I enjoyed some of the old "lost episodes" of The Jackie Gleason show. We laughed a lot at Ralph and Alice Kramden and Ed and

Trixie Norton, living life together in the Bronx. Like our most beloved stories, the Jackie Gleason Show had a common plot: Ralph, the poor bus driver who wants to make his wife proud of him, or find meaning in life in some way, cooks up a grandiose plan. He gets his buddy Ed, a happy-go-lucky city worker (in the sewers), to go along with him. Alice, wiser and more in tune with their actual condition even while she is as desirous as her husband at improving their lives, must put the brakes on. Ralph doesn't listen. He gets into trouble. We get *schadenfreude*—enjoyment of other people's misfortunes. But in the end, Ralph comes to Alice and confesses his scheme as bigger than his gifts. He admits that he wants something more for his wife. Alice understands. She receives him. And we are left with, sometimes, a tear for the big clown.

One of the most useful courses I ever took in seminary was on theological reflection—finding God in everyday life. As I watched Jackie Gleason that night with my family, I realized that I am so often like Ralph. I have some big plans. Now, I have never told my wife, "One day, Alice, right in the kisser!" or asked her, "Do you want to go to the moon?" but I have done some pretty boneheaded things in my life. Like Alice, my wife has been there. She has used her femininity to help me. She sees things I can't, including parts of myself that need shaping, and she is always there.

Like all great storylines, this is a gospel story. It features a prodigal who ends up powerless and depleted of resources and a loving God who is always there to welcome him home. It is the story of Jesus Christ, a God we can touch, the lover of our souls, who knows our motivations and who shapes us, not with coercion but rather with loving, divine patience. He puts up with our grandiose, Ralph-like plans, and then he loves us to the end.

I know that watching old Jackie Gleason shows isn't like watching a Billy Graham crusade, but as I watched these old episodes and thought about these things, I wanted to sing "Just As I Am."

45

OUT OF OUR MINDS

When they came to Jesus, they found the
man from whom the demons had gone out,
sitting at Jesus' feet, dressed and in his right
mind; and they were afraid. —Luke 8:35, NIV

The story of the man of the tombs, the insane savage who lived in the graves of the Gadarenes, is one of my favorite stories in the Bible. It wasn't always. You will remember that Jesus walked peaceably into the lair of the dead, into the haunted place where others feared to tread, and he mercifully but commandingly cast out the horrible demons from a tortured soul.

These demons had caused this poor fellow to become like a beast. He was a human savage. He was isolated. He hurt himself purposefully and repeatedly on the jagged stone edges of the tombs. He hated himself as much as others hated him. He lived among the dead, perhaps envying their condition. This one even sought to attack Jesus, but instead, Jesus transformed him.

The grace of Jesus was greater than all his sins. This dirty man became a clean man. This man, who was out of his mind, sat at Jesus' feet, taking the humble position of a disciple. I love the story because it reminds me of the power of God to change the worst of us. It reminds me, personally, of how God changed me. I am that man of the tombs.

- I once was isolated from human love by my own sin, living in the land of the dead, but now I am gathered in a community of eternal life called the church;
- I once hurt myself through the powers of hell that were at work within me, but now the tender love of Jesus and his acceptance is bringing healing to old wounds;
- I once sought to destroy the gospel I now desire to learn and to share with others;
- I once thought like a madman, but now I am beginning to be renewed in my thinking.

And all of this happened not because I went out and chose Jesus, but because he chose me. I was bound to the graveyard of my sins, but Jesus my Savior walked into my life and literally saved me.

To help you focus on the work of Jesus, picture in your mind a beautiful flower growing amidst the inhospitable environment of a granite rock mountain. Perhaps you have witnessed such a beautiful scene before in a photograph, or have been fortunate enough to see it in person. I think of the life of Jesus taking root and flowering in lives like that, lives like yours and mine. If you are like me, you couldn't imagine yourself to be the place where Jesus' beauty could take root. But that is grace.

46

Ain't Got No Kids?
Baloney!

Oh, you know about Miss Ee-ver" (Eva was pronounced Ee-ver, which rhymes with fever), one lady said to another, whispering, pointing, and trying to help her identify the poised, always-smiling, older woman pushing her grocery cart to the dairy section. I overheard the muted conversation behind the canned goods at the Red and White grocery store in Watson, Louisiana. "You know, that sweet woman who lives out there on the Fore Road, who ain't got no kids. Well, I mean, you know, she's got that orphan boy, but she ain't really got no kids." I was stunned.

"Ain't got no kids?" "Orphan boy?" Baloney! Sure she had a kid! She had me! And I was no orphan boy! I was, well, Eva Turner's boy! I might call her "Aunt Eva," but she was my mama and I had never known another! I was incensed. Through other such painful moments, I would soon learn the truth, that, like that one shortsighted lady who could only see family through the lens of her own experience, our "family" was not normal to many observers. I didn't know it until people like her informed me. Sadly, I would come to learn about how others thought of us—not only at the Red and White grocery store, but also at church.

As I listened and grew, I came to experience the pain that came with such insensitive utterances about my family. Mother's Day was sometimes a tough day for me, as it may be for some today. I think it might have been tough for Aunt Eva as well, but her faith in the God of miracles and her joy in his strength was stronger than mine. I think now that Mother's Day was probably her greatest day, for her Christ-centered faith and God-sent joy precluded self-pity, embarrassment, regrets, and everything else. God put us together as a family, and that was it. What had happened had happened. God was in control. He was working all things together for the good. Period.

On Mother's Day in our little rural community, when the song leader asked the mothers to stand— the newest mother, the mother with the most children, the oldest mother, and so forth and so on—he would always end by asking all mothers to stand. My Aunt Eva (the one of whom it was said "She ain't got no kids") then stood up quickly. And she stood proud. I can still see her smiling. She would look down at me, pat me with her Sunday white-gloved hand, and reassure me, without saying a word, that God had made us a family. She made me smile. She made me proud. I loved her so much. When she sat back down, I just wanted to put my head in her lap. Sometimes I did and slept through the rest of the service! I slept contented that God and our pastor—who always smiled biggest when Aunt Eva stood—understood.

Our pastor, Dr. Pierce, confirmed that Aunt Eva was my mother and convinced me that the wagging tongues of others were wrong. I was safe and happy. No matter what else happened in our lives, my mother was beside me. There would come days when I would lose my way, and those quiet, sacred moments would draw me back—back to Aunt Eva, back to learn the grace of God in Christ, which was the strength of her days.

I tell you this because every Mother's Day, each of us should honor our moms. We don't necessarily have to ask them to stand, but all of us, men and women, should take some time to think about how some woman—some mom—"stood up" for us in our lives.

Today, I want to honor mothers. Every woman is a gift of the Lord to others. You are the woman God has put here to show his nurturing love, reveal his caring heart, and show his tender mercies to his children who are in desperate need of experiencing it. Some of you have extended your mothering skills outside of your own family. Some of you are mothering little children who need a woman's tender touch. Some of you are being the woman that a little girl needs to look up to. Some of you are being mothers to aging gentlemen who are dying for the soft voice of a woman, like the voice of a wife now deceased, or the distant voice of grandmothers who reared them. You are God's woman for God's people. And if you are such a woman, you are a mother.

"Ain't got no kids?" Baloney! Every woman who puts her God-given skills to good use and allows the compassion and mercy of a loving Savior to shine through to others is fulfilling the high calling of a mother. Let us thank God for such women and for the ways they bless all of our lives.

47

FREE AT LAST!

I will not let go of Easter. More properly, I affirm that the resurrection of Jesus Christ is not something that I will celebrate and remember on one day of the year. In the Reformed faith, that is, the Protestant faith of Martin Luther and John Calvin and John Knox, the "high holy days" of the old Roman church were replaced with an understanding that each and every Lord's Day is a celebration of the resurrection of Jesus Christ. Every Sunday is Easter. What does that mean to us?

By this stage in these writings you know that I was orphaned and adopted by my father's sister, Aunt Eva Turner. I owe so much to her. If there is anything good about me or my ministry, I assure you—and I mean this with every fiber of my being—it must have come through her. You see, I believe in prayer more than I believe in genetics. I believe in an environment of love and hope and Christ more than I believe in a destiny determined by my bloodline. I thank God that his power can overcome the demonic strongholds that come into people's lives. If it were the other way around, I would be a castaway or in prison or worse. But God gave me Aunt Eva and I heard about Jesus from her. When my Aunt Eva fell ill, at almost 99 years of age, I watched her decline in just a few days until she died. I will never forget being there at her bedside and knowing that her spirit had left this place and was with Jesus Christ. I felt that a part of me was there. In a real way, I felt that she was free.

I read a story once about a Christian woman who was in much worse shape than my Aunt Eva was when she died. This older woman was confined to a bed in a nursing home. In order to keep her from falling out of bed, they strapped her in. Above her bed there was a sign that read, "This patient must be restrained at all times." This broke her dear daughter's heart, and every time her daughter went to see her, she wept as she saw that sign. She cried as her mother pleaded with her to untie the straps and set her free. One day her daughter was called in and told "Your mother died." When she walked into the room and saw her mother's body there, as a believer she knew the truth—her mother was not there. She was with Jesus. She ran and ripped that detestable sign off the wall, tore it up, and threw it away, saying, "Thank God, she is free at last!"[1]

I will not let go of Easter. Not yet. Not until the detestable graves are emptied of their sacred contents, not until the last tear has been shed, not until the vestige of sickness and disease and sorrow and affliction has been done away with. Not until Jesus comes.

1. Leighton Farrell, *Cries from the Cross* (Nashville: Abingdon Press, 1994), p. 95.

Then I will go into eternity with the words *He is risen* on my lips.

The resurrection of Jesus tells us that something is afoot. There is a new way of life that is taking over. The last enemy—death—will soon be destroyed, but for now, the fear, the sign above our heads that restrains us and holds us back and takes the joy of living away from us has been ripped away.

Thank God, we are free at last.

48

God Knows Your Name

I want to share with you a message that I gave to orphans in Tirana, Albania. I delivered the message to them in Albanian, but it is in English for you. My prayer is that you who are searching for identity will find it, as I wanted these children to do, and as I finally did in the Lord himself.

It is my great honor to be with you this evening. My name is Michael Milton and this is my son John Michael. I bring you greetings from our church, First Presbyterian Church, in Chattanooga, Tennessee.

You and I have something in common. I was an orphan. I was reared by my aunt in a rural, poverty-stricken area of Louisiana in the United States. As I grew up, I began to have problems understanding my identity. I had great pain in my heart. That pain led me on a search for meaning. In that search I made many mistakes. But a person is never so far from God that

God cannot find him. Jesus said, "I have come to seek the lost." I thank God he found me!

One of the things that changed my life for the better was coming to know that God knew my name. Isaiah 43:1 says: "But now thus says the LORD, he who created you, O Jacob, he who formed you, O Israel: 'Fear not, for I have redeemed you; I have called you by name, you are mine.'" God had created me. He had formed me. Just as he called Jacob and from him made a great nation called Israel, so God made me. In Jesus Christ I have found my true identity.

The apostle Paul preached in the land God had given the Israelites. Romans tells us, "So from Jerusalem all the way around to Illyricum, I have fully proclaimed the gospel of Christ" (15:19, NIV). Paul was a man whose identity could have been built on the pain of guilt brought about from his former life of persecuting others. After he came to know Christ and the power of a new identity, he wrote these words: "Therefore, if anyone is in Christ, he is a new creation; the old has gone, the new has come!" (2 Corinthians 5:17, NIV).

So I believe God has sent me to you, as one of you, to tell you God loves you. He made you. He created you. He knows you by name. Don't ever forget that. Know that God has sent his Son Jesus Christ to find you, to show the fullness of God's love for you, by going to the extreme point of loneliness and pain on a cross as a sacrifice for your sins, so that you can become the adopted son or daughter of God.

That is what the Lord Jesus did for me. He does it for anyone who will receive him as Lord and Savior.

49

How Marylu Baxter's Cinnamon Rolls Saved My Soul

For we are to God the aroma of Christ
among those who are being saved.
—2 Corinthians 2:15a, NIV

I can smell them now! Sweet, buttery, rich, hot, sticky, thick and crowded together, plump, freshly baked, and hot right out of the oven! How I love Marylu Baxter's cinnamon rolls! So would you if you could just taste one! You would never be the same again!

Sunday nights in Olathe in the 1980s were a time of growth for Mae and me. That growth came from Marylu Baxter's cinnamon rolls. You guessed it; there was a lot of growth around my middle section because of those delicious one-of-a-kind Kansas creations by the woman whom I consider to be the Queen of the Cinnamon Roll—our pastor's wife, Marylu. But there was much more.

Growth in Fellowship

Pastor Bob Baxter's greatest asset, like any other happily married man, is his wife. The ministry of Marylu Baxter enhances the ministry of Robert Baxter. How does she do it? God uses many gifts, but in her case, Marylu knows how to cook—not just cinnamon rolls but strawberry-rhubarb pie and everything else as well. This woman just has the gift of hospitality. She would invariably catch people before Sunday night worship (practically every Sunday) and say, "Why don't you come on over and eat? We've got plenty." She always did. After visiting just once, I don't think we ever said no. The warm Midwestern kitchen of that pastor's home had an aroma that drew many into contact with Pastor Bob, his family, and other church members. The nourishment and simple pleasure of food was the centerpiece for fellowship.

Now when I say fellowship, I certainly mean fun and laughter and the pure enjoyment of other human beings. But at their house it meant all that plus fellowship in Jesus Christ. You may know that one of my favorite apostolic blessings is "May the grace of the Lord Jesus Christ, and the love of God, and the fellowship of the Holy Spirit be with you all" (2 Corinthians 13:14, NIV). Maybe this is because at their house I encountered the fellowship of the Holy Spirit in a way I had never known before. Even now, well over a decade later, such fellowship in Christ still lingers in my heart like the magical aroma of those fresh cinnamon rolls right out of the oven.

So we grew in fellowship during those days. That fellowship strengthened us. It made us see the beauty of the church of Jesus Christ, helped us to see how to relate to other believers, showed us how to share our own lives with others, and taught us how to listen as others shared what God was doing in their lives.

Growth in Family

Those evenings eating at Marylu's table taught me how to be a husband, a father, and a friend. To this day I consider Pastor Bob and Marylu to be my spiritual father and mother, and I consider their children to be my siblings in the faith—Mary and her husband, Kent; Mark and his wife, Janet; and Jim (who was away at seminary during that time and now pastors the church his father planted in Olathe, Kansas) and his wife, Wendy. Pastor Bob never said, "Alright, tonight I will begin lesson one in being a husband." He just lived it. Right there in front of us. Effortlessly. Faithfully.

At one Fourth of July picnic, Mae, Amy, Aunt Eva, and I were with the Baxters. We were eating at a park, dining as usual on Marylu's delicacies. Aunt Eva was lifting her fork to her mouth with a piece of cinnamon roll on it when a good, strong Kansas wind came up and blew her fork away! She was left with her hand to her mouth with nothing in it! Pastor Bob roared with laughter, and then Aunt Eva bent over in giggles. We all laughed and talked about that day for many years to come. That day I saw firsthand that family was filled with some beautiful moments even when the cinnamon rolls were blown away. I see that image in my mind now, and I am reminded that in Christ, laughter is good and is especially needed when sudden winds come and take sweet things from you.

221

Growth in Faith

Aunt Eva told me, "I have lived ninety-seven years and Pastor Bob is the best pastor and preacher I have ever known." She meant it. Of course, there are many great preachers and wonderful pastors, but I guess she said that because he was the pastor God gave us. It was not so much that we found a pastor that we liked, but that God knew the pastor we needed and he brought us to him.

I first heard the gospel of grace from D. James Kennedy at an Evangelism Explosion conference. I was also introduced to the Reformed faith and to the Presbyterian Church in America. When I moved to Kansas City because of a promotion with Ashland Chemical Company, I knew I had to find a church that preached that message. So God led me to Pastor Bob.

He taught me that the truth of the Scriptures is that our chief end is to glorify God and to enjoy him. Pastor Bob enjoys God. If anyone knows him, they know that. I still recall his prayers before Sunday night meals: "Lord, thank you for the appetite you have given us! If we didn't have that, we couldn't enjoy this wonderful food you have given us!" He taught me that everything—*everything*—is related to the Lord and his goodness. His sovereignty and his grace are to be found in every moment.

Thus, through Marylu's wonderful cinnamon rolls, every Lord's Day was capped off with sweet, rich, warm fellowship, family, and faith. I learned to thank God for the gift of an appetite for him. I will never, ever be able to thank Pastor Bob and Marylu enough for that. I pray that I can pass along to others what they taught me: the aroma of Christ Jesus.

50

GIVING OUR
CHILDREN TO GOD

*I prayed for this child, and the LORD has
granted me what I asked of him. So now I
give him to the LORD. For his whole life he
will be given over to the LORD. —I Samuel
1:27–28a NIV*

*H*ave you given your children to God?
    I went to minister to a child, but as usual
in cases such as this she ministered to me. A
call came from a PCA pastor at a sister congregation in
Wichita, Kansas: "One of our families has a daughter
who has been in a car wreck. She is having multiple
operations. The mom and dad are living in the Ronald
McDonald House. They have been through so much.
Mike, could you go and visit?" I took Ray Barrett (our

interim assistant) with me. We were able to pray at the foot of their daughter's bed.

After four operations on her skull she looked remarkably good. She was sleeping. Our prayers were silent. When we left her room we found out the family had been up all night. I felt that we should try to visit them, if possible. The fine folks at the Ronald McDonald House welcomed us and informed the family that we were there. The mother came down and introduced herself. She bore that kind of fresh, country, meat-and-potatoes Midwestern persona that I remember so well from my years of living there. She told us the prognosis looked so much better now and they were able to sleep the sleep of relief.

As we sat we heard about the call they had received at two in the morning. It was the kind of call that no parent wants. "Does your daughter drive a such and such vehicle?" "Yes." "Well, there has been an accident . . ." And in that moment, a million things went through their minds. Time stopped. When they asked about their daughter's condition, there was not a confirmation that she was alive.

The mother told me that she asked God, "Lord, what do I pray? Do I pray that my daughter is alive? If so, it sounds like another parent's child could be dead." She said that right then her faith, a gift of God, involuntarily kicked in. "Lord, my daughter is your daughter. She has received you by faith. She trusts in Jesus and his finished work on Calvary. Lord, if my child is not here, I know where she is. I have given her to you. I do not know about the spiritual state of the other children. Lord, my child is not my own. She is yours." And with that, she comforted herself in the Lord.

She told me that as she waited for confirmation from the doctors in those next few moments, her soul was at peace. It was a peace born of faith and a faith given by God, not manufactured in her mind. Then the word came back: "Ma'am, your daughter is alive. She is in critical condition. But she is alive." We talked about how she hung up the phone and again released her daughter into the hands of God for his healing.

As I write this, I tell you that I have rarely been in the presence of a more genuine, godly, and peace-filled human being. We prayed, and in my heart I prayed for myself. I prayed that I would be able to pray, "Lord, my child is not my own. He is yours."

This is what Hannah prayed. She had longed for a child. God gave her Samuel. But immediately, upon his birth, she returned him to the Lord.

Will you pray with me? "O dear heavenly Father, that we may all release our loved ones to you. May we all learn to cherish the gifts you give us, whatever or whomever they may be, and then release them back to you in an act of worship."

51

HA ERETS, THE MIDWEST, AND HEAVEN IN MY SOUL

I was given the privilege of speaking at the annual Bible conference in Cedar Falls, Iowa, during the summer. They hold it at a campground just like they have since the turn of the last century. Some of the same families who were there when these hearty, godly Midwesterners gathered to hear the early evangelists and guest pastors are still there today.

I like preaching there because I like Midwesterners. I have been married to one for a quarter of a century, my son spent his first years on the Midwestern landscape, and I found a new life there. Just like the pioneers before me, I journeyed there to start a new life. The old one hadn't worked out very well. Now, I didn't choose to become a Midwesterner (you can become one, though it is generally thought that one cannot become a Southerner or a New Englander). I chose something else.

The earlier settlers on the land probably didn't say, "Living in Minnesota would be really neat." No. You go to the prairie because there is the promise of a new life there. It is the new life that you are seeking. That is what Willa Cather wrote about, I believe, in all of her stories about pioneering families. Life and land became so intertwined that they are symbols for each other. Well, our story is no "My Antonia" or "Neighbor Rosicky" or "O Pioneers!", but God sent us to the Midwest and there is a story there.

I will never forget arriving there. I was 27 years old, and it was in the fall. I was staying in a hotel my company had arranged for me, located on the edge of a suburban sprawl. I didn't know what suburban sprawl was, but I liked it. I had never seen houses so nicely arranged as those in Overland Park, Kansas, where the green, groomed corporate business parks touched the vast, cultivated rows in fields. On that first morning there I felt like the land was drawing me in, across the business parks, away from the route to my new office.

I drove until I couldn't see anything but fields to the north, south, east, and west. I parked my car, got out, and felt the Midwest prairie wind as it chilled me to the bone. I liked it. It was not like the pneumonia-wet 32-degree air of New Orleans. It felt cleaner, crisper, and it even gave me a slight ache in the lungs, almost a laceration, when I sucked it in. I carefully crossed a ditch and stood next to a fence line. I just stood there. I was now part of this new land. My soul was still newly born from an encounter with God's grace. I thought about it: "Here I am, a poor kid from Louisiana, my life broken and battered by my own sins and the sins of

228

others, on my way up the corporate ladder of success, married to the greatest gal in the world, and now led by God to be a part of this land. This land."

I stood beneath a November Kansas sky that seemed bigger than any sky I had ever seen in my whole life. Standing in wonder on the fence line of the most magnificent field I had ever seen, I felt like I was home. I had a drawing pad in the car and some colored pencils, so, lacking a camera, I drew the field, including the Hereford cattle grazing in the distance. Then it began to snow. I was undeterred and even rather encouraged by the scene. I was drawing the land and the sky (sky being the predominant feature of the land there), with one pencil clinched in my chattering teeth and my car running with its blue exhaust swirling all around me. That drawing is somewhere in our home, but the scene of the fields and the sky is forever etched into my soul. The Midwest. My Midwest. My prairie. No, I guess not. God's land; God's prairie.

Since that time, I have moved around, answering calls, serving the church sort of like a soldier serves the army and goes from assignment to assignment. I live in North Carolina now. But my soul is forever shaped by that gray November Kansas sky and that vast frozen field I took into my soul that first day when I stepped onto the Midwest prairie. I am—and I think I always will be—a Midwesterner.

In the Hebrew, there is a word, *ha erets*, the land. The land is where we were meant to be. Genesis tells us,

In the beginning, God created the heavens and [ha erets, the land]. (Genesis 1:1)

229

[Ha erets, the land,] brought forth vegetation, plants yielding seed according to their own kinds, and trees bearing fruit in which is their seed, each according to its kind. And God saw that it was good. (1:12)

In our sin, the land is what we lost.

When you work the ground, it shall no longer yield to you its strength. You shall be a fugitive and a wanderer on [ha erets, the land]. (Genesis 4:12)

In his goodness and grace, God promised a return to the land.

Now the LORD said to Abram, "Go from your country and your kindred and your father's house to [ha erets, the land,] that I will show you." (Genesis 12:1)

And so the covenant-bearer, Abram, heard the divine command of promise.

Arise, walk through the length and the breadth of [ha erets, the land,] for I will give it to you. (Genesis 13:17)

Of course the land was lost, in sin. It always is lost here. What I learned was that in God's grace, ha erets, the land, is a living sign of the redemption we have in Jesus Christ. Ha erets, the land, is where we are going in him. It is not just heaven; it is heaven in our souls. And it is a real promise of a new heaven and a new earth. For we were meant to tend the garden in ha erets, the land.

When I preach at the Cedar Falls Bible Conference in Iowa, I taste the bratwursts, the flesh of ha erets, and the boiled corn, the grain of ha erets, and watch the children chasing fireflies in the dusk of the day, glimpses of future glory-days in ha erets. I look past the white clapboard houses of the old Bible campgrounds to the golden August fields that lie just beyond the fence lines as they always must in this life. I look out and taste ha erets with my eyes, and drink in its truth like a thirsty child lapping at the cold water trickling from a green garden hose on a hot summer day.

I am ready for ha erets. The older I get the more I want to be there. I know it sounds funny to some, but ha erets is now a place in my soul, a Midwestern place, a holy place.

It is good to go back, and to preach the gospel of the One who is leading us home, and to be reminded of the ha erets for which I am really longing.

52

WHERE DID YOU MEET GOD TODAY?

That very day two of them were going to a
village named Emmaus, about seven miles
from Jerusalem, and they were talking with
each other about all these things that had
happened. While they were talking and
discussing together, Jesus himself drew near
and went with them. —Luke 24:13–15

I just read a quote by Dorothy Bass from her "Receiving the Day" (as it appears in *Christianity
Today,* March 2006, p. 67):

"How was your day?" A mother I know has a different way of asking the same question. As she tucks
her children into bed each night . . . she asks them
a question: "Where did you meet God today?" And

they tell her, one by one: A teacher helped me; there was a homeless person in the park; I saw a tree with lots of flowers in it. She tells them where she met God, too. Before the children drop off to sleep, the stuff of the day has become the substance of their prayer.

Am I more like the disciples on the road to Emmaus, not discerning the presence of Jesus in my journey today, or more like those children in Dorothy Bass's story?

Today I met God when one of our *Faith for Living* radio program listeners e-mailed me to ask me to pray for his wife, who had breast cancer. I remember meeting God in prayer as I agonized with a hurting husband. I met God as my son came to me with his new braces. He was eager for me to see him. He was so happy about this moment (strange as it may seem) that we both went into a three-point stance and started hitting each other like two football linemen after a snap. (Yes, that may seem strange too, but this is what we do when we are happy.) I met God when I met with a young man who doesn't want his wife to leave him. And I met God when I prayed with one of our staff members. The Lord was there when my wife laughed. It seems he is always there when she smiles.

Then there were some friends of John Michael's who came to our house. They hid from me, and as I walked in the door, they tried to scare me. I remember sensing God's presence as I met with some women in our church who are dreaming dreams of ministry. Jessica, my deaf daughter who is a psychologist at the Louisiana School for the Deaf, e-mailed me a picture of her little boy Eli, who signed "I love you" to Poppy (me). I teared up and felt the hand of God on my shoulder reminding me of his goodness. This afternoon I prayed with a widow. I remember thinking, "Lord, I need your help." He was there in that moment.

This evening I embraced one of our members at a visitation at the funeral home. In her tears, I recalled the tears of Jesus at the tomb of Lazarus. It seemed good and right that she wept as she did. I wanted to cry too. I knelt to listen to her mother tell me, "I know where he (her husband) is." I prayed with them and reminded them of the resurrection. And the Lord was there too. I have only just begun to recount his appearances.

Funny. I might have missed those moments if I had not been asked, "Where did you meet God today?" How many roads to Emmaus have I walked with him and missed him? How many nights have the sacred moments of life been wasted? How many times have I thought about how my day went, rather than how he went with me through this day?

But not this time. This time, by his grace, the stuff of the day has become the substance of prayer. Thank you, Lord. It is going to make for a sweeter night and a fresher tomorrow.

Where did you meet God today?

God bless you.

COMING SOON FROM P&R

Price: $14.99
To order, visit www.prpbooks.com
Or call 1(800) 631-0094

To truly love God we must know him.

Not just know that he exists, but know who he is and what he is like. What better way to do this than to study what God declares about himself in his own Word?

This exploration of God's unchanging character, as revealed in thirteen stories from the Bible, offers you an opportunity to get to know him better and love him more. Each chapter focuses on a different attribute of God, how it influences your understanding of him, and how you can apply it to your daily life.

"It takes peculiar skill to provide an explanation of God's attributes that both feeds the mind and stirs the heart. Phil Ryken achieves this and more in this most helpful book."

—Alistair Begg

ALSO BY MICHAEL A. MILTON

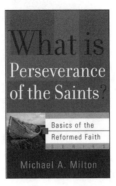

Price: $3.99
To order, visit www.prpbooks.com
Or call 1(800) 631-0094

Mike Milton explains this doctrine with sensitivity and clarity, distinguishes it from other theologies (including "once saved always saved"), and encourages all of us to delight as it brings assurance to the believer, hope for the prodigal, and glory to the Lord Jesus Christ.

"This truth of the perseverance of the saints, which entails the final security of believers, is a profoundly practical point of Scripture truth. Mike Milton knows that, and explains and applies it to you in a wonderfully instructive and compelling way."
—Ligon Duncan

"Mike Milton thinks like a scholar, but writes like a pastor. He takes subtle issues and, without dumbing them down, explains them in easy-to-understand terms. That is a wonderful gift to the church."
—Joel Belz